The Stress-free Gui
Studying at Unive

The Stress-free Guide to Studying at University

A Student's Guide Towards a Better Life

Gordon Rugg, Sue Gerrard and Susie Hooper

Los Angeles • London • New Delhi • Singapore

SAGE Publications Ltd
1 Oliver's Yard
55 City Road
London EC1Y 1SP

SAGE Publications Inc.
2455 Teller Road
Thousand Oaks, California 91320

SAGE Publications India Pvt Ltd
B 1/I 1 Mohan Cooperative Industrial Area
Mathura Road, Post Bag 7
New Delhi 110 044

SAGE Publications Asia-Pacific Pte Ltd
33 Pekin Street #02-01
Far East Square
Singapore 048763

Library of Congress Control Number: 2007932196

British Library Cataloguing in Publication data

A catalogue record for this book is available from the British Library

ISBN 978-1-4129-4492-2
ISBN 978-1-4129-4493-9 (pbk)

Typeset by C&M Digital Pvt Ltd, Chennai, India
Printed in Great Britain by The Cromwell Press Ltd, Trowbridge, Wiltshire
Printed on paper from sustainable resources

Contents

Preface

Does the world need another book about stress? What this book is, and what it does for you.

Although the world may be short of many things, it's unlikely to suffer a shortage of books about stress in the foreseeable future. So why this book? We've written it to bring together several strands of student life which are usually handled in separate books. One is stress; another is the academic world; a third is student life. This book brings these three strands together, and also shows how to move from stress to positive well-being.

The introductory chapter is about stress itself. The next chapter is about ways of handling stress. The remainder of the book is structured around the main stressors and stresses which can be expected in a taught degree – for instance, adjustment in the first semester, financial difficulties and the pressure of final examinations at the end of the degree. Each chapter explains the key relevant issues, suggests ways of reducing or preventing problems, and gives advice about handling the stressor and about moving on afterwards. In addition, there is a chapter on stressors and stresses which are particularly likely to affect groups of students traditionally marginalised by the academic system, such as mature students with young families, part-time students and overseas students.

We've included real life examples. These are all based on actual cases, but we've changed details such as the students' names and courses to preserve their anonymity. All the examples are true, however unlikely some of them might appear. We hope you'll find this book useful, and that it will help you towards happiness.

1

Stress and well-being: an overview

(or, What is stress anyway, and what better things does life hold?)

'Stress' and related concepts. What stress is. The stress response: its good and bad points. Handling stress via the three-stage strategy: prevention, management and moving on. Well-being.

At some point in their life, almost everyone goes through pain and unpleasantness and stress. That's what this book is about. It's structured around three main strategies. One involves reducing the likelihood of bad things hitting you. The second involves ways to handle bad situations when they do happen. The third is for learning from bad experiences and going on to achieve positive well-being in your life. You might be reading this book because you're going through a bad time right now. If so, the next chapter contains some exercises and tactics for immediate fixes that will keep you going while you sort out longer-lasting solutions. If you're in a very bad situation, then Appendix 1 contains a checklist for handling serious situations.

This chapter is about the thing which people generally call 'stress.' That's a useful term for everyday use but, like most everyday terms, it has its limitations when you want to go into more detail. The popular conception is that stress is a thing, like high blood pressure, a single homogeneous condition, so that every case of stress shares the same underlying features, just as every case of high blood pressure shares the same key features. The reality is more complex, and if you're dealing with a situation which you find stressful, then it's best to know something about the underlying detail. That's what this chapter is about. Once you understand what you're dealing with, you're in a much better position for dealing with it.

There are some things that this book doesn't do and can't do. It's not a do-it-yourself psychotherapy book; that's a different topic, and one better handled via face-to-face encounters with a human being who has been trained in that area, rather than via a book. Nor is it a handbook offering The One True Answer on every aspect of your life, including legal issues. A key point is that often in life there isn't a single 'right' answer; learning to accept that fact is an important part of growth and development. This book isn't the whole answer, but it does bring together a set of concepts which should help you towards a happier and more fulfilled life. The rest of this chapter is about what stress is and what it isn't; the following chapter is about things you can do about stress.

'STRESS' AND RELATED CONCEPTS

There are various feelings that overlap with stress. One obvious one is anxiety; another is depression; a third is panic; a fourth is phobias. We'll describe each of these briefly before going on to stress itself.

Anxiety is an unpleasant mix of feelings, often including uneasiness, distress, worry and low-level fear. Anxiety is often about a specific thing, about meeting a particular person or about an anticipated event, like an exam. Sometimes, though, it isn't about anything in particular, and involves a shapeless, nameless dread; this variant is known as 'free-floating anxiety.'

Depression is a persistent feeling of gloom and dejection, with a persistent lowness of mood and energy. It is often caused by loss of a person, whether through death, separation or the end of a relationship. It is more intense than ordinary unhappiness and having a bad day; if you're experiencing normal unhappiness and some unexpected good news arrives, then you'll probably snap out of the unhappiness and start enjoying the good news, whereas if you're experiencing depression, unexpected good news won't make much difference to your mood. A related condition is Seasonal Affective Disorder (SAD), which can make you feel depressed, lethargic and generally low during a particular season (usually winter, in the case of the northern hemisphere). This condition is not yet well understood, but appears to involve a physiological response to reduced sunlight; it usually improves if you get more sunlight or full-spectrum artificial light.

Panic is a feeling of overwhelming dread and anxiety, coupled with palpitations, sweating, and feeling faint, out of control and unreal. The feeling does not last long, but panic attacks can be vividly remembered, and can be linked with phobias. Sometimes the fear of another attack leads people to avoid the situation where the first attack happened; for instance, having a panic attack while in one large store led to one client avoiding all large shops.

Phobias involve an irrational fear of something; this is often accompanied by panic attacks if the feared object is present. Common phobias include fear of snakes, spiders, cats and heights. Phobias differ in strength; it's possible to be only mildly phobic about something. The key feature is that the fear is irrational; many people with phobias deny that their fear is irrational (for instance, being afraid of spiders is not inherently silly, given that many countries have spiders capable of injuring or killing an adult). However, someone with a spider phobia is likely to react fearfully to pictures of spiders, toy spiders, or even the word 'spider.'

WHAT IS STRESS?

The usual descriptions of stress involve something happening (the stressor) and the body responding with some predictable physiological and psycholog-ical reactions (the stress response). These reactions make evolutionary sense, since they're fairly good for immediate, life-threatening physical dangers where you have a choice between fighting something as hard as you can or running away as fast as you can (the 'fight or flight' response). The trouble is that the stress reactions don't work very well for long-term, low-key threats, which are much more common in everyday life – the stress reactions don't give you the right type of support for these, and also tend to burn you out if they're sustained for too long. So, what is the stress response, and what does it do?

The stress response – what it is, what it does
The popular version is that when you feel stressed, the body dumps a load of stress chemicals into the bloodstream, and these super-charge you for a short period, then burn you out if the stress continues. As you might imag-ine, the full story is somewhat more complex, but the popular version is a useful starting point. When you feel stressed, the body does indeed dump a load of stress chemicals into your bloodstream. These have various effects which can be useful in some dangerous situations, though they're not always useful. For instance, people in dangerous situations often don't notice pain, which can sometimes be very helpful (since it lets you concen-trate on getting out of the situation, or fixing it) and can sometimes be very maladaptive (since you could be unaware of a life-threatening injury). Other effects include the following:

- heart-rate, blood pressure and sweating increase
- digestion slows so that blood from the stomach can be diverted to the muscles and brain
- breathing becomes fast and shallow
- muscles tense in preparation for action
- the blood forms clots more rapidly
- sugars and fats are released into the blood for rapid release of energy; this gives strength and endurance in an emergency.

Unfortunately for would-be Incredible Hulks, the effects don't include superhuman strength, despite the urban legends, though there may be cases where people exert more strength than they normally would, since they don't notice the pain which results from them over-exerting themselves.

One part of the brain involved in the stress response is the amygdala, a small structure shaped like an almond and located near the base of the brain. Other parts of the body involved include the adrenal glands (situated above your kidneys), stomach and lungs. Your pancreas and liver are involved in regulating the sugars circulating in your blood, which are burned to supply energy. In stressful situations, your muscles tense up, so you are ready to take action.

Problems with the stress response

The stress response is fine if you want a short burst of furious energy while you focus on one goal. It's not so good if you need a long, steady stream of moderate energy, or if you need to think clearly so you can choose the right goal in the first place. The stress response can be precipitated by a variety of situations.

Frustration typically occurs when people are prevented from doing what they want. Frustration results in feelings of being ineffectual, discouraged and demotivated. Individuals vary in their tolerance of frustration. If a frustrating situation continues, the individual involved may slip into learned helplessness.

Learned helplessness is something that can occur with long-term stress, when there is no visible way of escaping from an unpleasant situation. People stop struggling against the situation, and will often not attempt to escape even when an apparent way out is offered. This may look to an outsider as if the individual has become happy with the situation, but in reality the individual has reached the point where they believe that further efforts will only result in further disappointments which are even worse than the present situation.

Post-Traumatic Stress Disorder (PTSD) is usually associated with a major traumatic event, such as a natural disaster, car accident, rape or other serious crime. The event is experienced in a very distressing way, and is associated with fear, terror, bewilderment and a sense of helplessness. The symptoms can include reliving the events as flashbacks or dreams, intrusive thoughts about the event, sleep disturbances, feeling guilty about the event and feeling guilty about having survived it if other people haven't. PTSD is usually associated with specific events, rather than the sort of long-term stressors that lead to frustration and learned helplessness.

Cognitive tunnel vision involves becoming focused on one part of the stressful situation, to such an extent that you lose sight of other relevant issues, and lose all sense of perspective. This typically takes the form of focusing on a relatively minor aspect of the problem while ignoring bigger and more important aspects.

Appropriateness of response is another issue in stressful situations. The physiological effects of the stress response set you up for a 'fight or flight' response, and for swift action, but often these are not the most appropriate response in the modern world; often you're better off calming down and assessing the situation objectively. This, however, is hard to do when there are stress hormones charging round your body trying to make it do just the opposite of calming down and being objective.

Artificial ecstasy is one common maladaptive strategy for handling stressful situations. This is a term we've borrowed from theology, not a term from the drugs culture. Artificial ecstasy is pleasure that is the emotional equivalent of junk food, giving you a short-term high, but storing up long-term problems. A typical example is someone whose everyday life is grotty and miserable, and who turns to drink, drugs or adrenal sports as a way of escaping from reality for a while into somewhere that's more pleasant while it lasts. The problem is that it doesn't last, and that it can store up more problems for you when you emerge. For instance, getting drunk might take your mind off your problems for an hour or two, but if you wake up in Accident and Emergency after a binge, then you're worse off than when you started. The opposite of this is natural ecstasy, when your reality is pleasant, so there's no need to think about escaping from it; that's what well-being is about, and a lot of this book is about how to achieve that sort of positive well-being.

Attribution effects are another common psychological issue in stressful situations. It's easy to blame the stressful situation on yourself, thereby lowering your self-esteem and making it more difficult for you to handle the situation well; conversely, some people tend automatically to blame stressful situations on other people, which again reduces the likelihood of assessing the situation realistically and deciding what the underlying cause is and what you should do about it: for instance, whether you need to change some of your behaviours.

Expressive and instrumental behaviour are extremely useful concepts. Expressive behaviour is about showing people what sort of person you are; instrumental behaviour is about getting something done. Each type of behaviour has its place, and each can cause problems when used in the wrong place. For instance, sitting in the library late at night looking miserable shows the world that you care about an assignment, but it isn't as much practical use as carrying out a sensibly planned strategy for getting the assignment done on time. Conversely, if someone has just heard that their favourite uncle has died, then their immediate need will be for some sympathetic emotional support rather than practical advice about travel arrangements to the funeral. It's easy to give up and lapse into expressive behaviour under stress, rather than examining the situation instrumentally and seeing whether you can fix it.

'STRESS' AS A CONCEPT

The problems with 'stress' as a concept

So far, we've been treating 'stress' as if it were a single, tangible condition, like a broken leg or a cold. The reality is more complex. 'Stress' is a useful simplification, but when you start to examine it more closely, you realise that it has its limitations. An obvious issue is that people differ widely in regard to what they find stressful; for instance, some people enjoy the adrenal thrill of public speaking, whereas others find it terrifying. There are some common features in what people find stressful, but these features involve psychological perceptions rather than objective attributes of the stressors – for example, people tend to find uncertainty and lack of control stressful. Stress researchers are well aware of these individual differences, and have tended to look beyond these into the underlying issues. One common underlying issue is that people often become stressed because of system problems, such as a job specification which nobody has any realistic chance of achieving, or an organisational structure which produces inevitable conflict between parts of the organisation. When people in these situations become stressed, there is a tendency for the organisation to treat this as a sign of weakness on the part of the individuals, rather than as a sign of poor organisational structure. This is a theme to which we return throughout the book.

Once the stress response kicks in, it's fairly standard across individuals. The physiology of the stress response is well understood, and there are plenty of well-established techniques for handling it. Chapter 2 deals with this topic. Handling the stress response is all very well, but it's important to make sure that you don't just move out of one stressful episode and straight into another. Also, there's more to life than just trying to dodge stress; life should contain positively good things, rather than simply an absence of bad things. There's an increasing amount of research into people's life strategies and into well-being; this is another theme to which we return throughout this book. An important part of well-being is the recognition that life contains bad times as well as good; true well-being includes knowing that you have the strategies and inner resources to face and to handle the bad times when they arise, so that you can move on from them in the direction that you want.

THE THREE-STEP STRATEGY

Most books about stress are intended for everybody, which limits their scope for specific advice about situations that lead to stress. With this book, we're writing for one group of people, namely undergraduates, so there's scope for giving specific advice about common causes of problems, about the problems themselves, and also about how to handle them. We've done this via a three-step strategy. The first step is to prevent problems where possible;

the second step is to have strategies ready for dealing with any that get past the initial defences, and the third step is to learn the right lessons from dealing with problems, so you can have a good life. The next three sections work through this in more detail.

Prevention

Sometimes bad things happen through no fault of your own: for instance, if a roof tile falls off a building onto your head. Other times, bad things happen because we don't have all the information we need: for example, nobody's told you the differences in preferred writing style between Psychology and Business Studies before your first assessment. Often, though, our own habits lead to problems which are fairly predictable: for instance, if you always leave things to the last minute, it's scarcely surprising if you eventually incur the wrath of The System for missing a deadline. (What is 'The System'? We've used this term (with capitals) as an abbreviation for the procedures, regulations and customs of an institution.)

There's not much anyone can do about preventing the 'no conceivable fault' things, but it's possible to do a lot about the 'missing information' things, and the later chapters contain assorted useful information which doesn't usually appear in departmental handbooks. It's also possible to do something about your own habits, if you're genuinely willing to make that happen. There's information about how to do this later on in this chapter and in Chapter 8.

Handling the situation

When you feel stressed, physiology kicks in, and there is a set of fairly standard mental and physical responses that occur. Some of these can be handled using the same techniques regardless of the original cause: for example, using deep, slow breathing to regulate your heart rate. Others are best handled in relation to the original cause. For instance, if you're feeling stressed because you don't understand what your lecturers expect in your coursework, then the appropriate strategy is to ask someone who can give you the information you need rather than to do the relaxation exercises. That leads on to the issue of how to move on from stress into well-being, which is the topic of the next section.

Moving on, and well-being

Back in the past, people who wrote about stress tended to view it as being like illness; something which came along from the outside, and which had a bad effect on you. When the illness had been driven out, you returned to the state you were in before the illness, and were then considered to be cured. Nowadays stress researchers are more likely to take a broader view, and to consider issues such as whether your original state might have contained some room for improvement and for positive well-being, as opposed to just the absence of any obvious stressors.

Bad situations are like accidentally landing your car in a ditch. The obvious next step is to get the car out of the ditch, back onto the road. Once it's on the road, and you're sure it's roadworthy, the wise thing to do is to understand why it went into the ditch in the first place, so that you can reduce the likelihood of ending up back in the ditch again. If it went in because you hit a patch of black ice while doing a sensible speed, then that's something that could happen to anyone, and there's a limited amount you can learn. If it went in because you were going too fast round a bend because you were worried about being late for a meeting, then there's quite a lot you can do. You can learn to drive more carefully round bends; you can also learn to allow more time for journeys; you can learn to worry less about being late for meetings. You can also ask yourself whether you really want to travel along that road in the first place. Similarly, it's one thing to abandon an academic course because of fear of failure, or because of feelings of inadequacy; it's a very different thing to make a calm, informed decision that you've tried the course and it's not for you. Sometimes the answer is to try a different course; sometimes the answer is to leave university and do something different.

Decisions like this are difficult for you to make, and are also difficult for other people to advise you about. There's a grey, difficult line for counsellors and other professionals, between what the client (e.g. you) asks for and what the counsellor thinks that the client actually needs, especially if the client is stressed out and afraid of taking on too much change.

Paradoxically, well-being can often appear threatening, because it can involve change, and people tend to find change threatening unless it's very clearly under their control. There's a story which is probably true about the time when a gale blew down some trees around the wolf enclosure at a zoo, destroying the fence. The zoo staff had horrible visions of the wolves ranging wild across the surrounding countryside, intoxicated with new-found freedom. What the staff found instead was the wolves cowering in the middle of their enclosure, ready to fight off any hideous threat that came in over the flattened fence into their nice familiar home. It's similar with people; a dull but familiar lifestyle can feel a lot more comfortable at first than a more enjoyable but unfamiliar new lifestyle. There's more about this in the next chapter.

SUMMARY

Stress isn't a single condition; different people find different things stressful. Stress isn't necessarily bad; it's often a temporary side-effect of change for the better. This book uses a three-stage strategy for handling stress. The first stage is preventing unhealthy stress if possible. The second is handling the stress reaction if it occurs. The third is moving on from stress towards positive well-being.

BIBLIOGRAPHY AND SUGGESTED FURTHER RESOURCES

There's a substantial literature on stress, ranging from introductory paperbacks through to heavyweight academic articles. The emphasis of this literature has changed over time. Earlier literature tended to assume that there was a clearly identifiable condition called 'stress' and to describe ways that the individual could deal with stress via methods such as relaxation. The later literature paid more attention to the bigger picture within which the stress was occurring, and looked at things like how organisational structures interacted with stress – for instance, some job specifications will inevitably put the individual into a difficult or impossible situation, which will almost inevitably make them feel stressed (or make them resign). Another later theme was whether there actually was a single thing that could be called 'stress' or whether the wide differences in what individuals found stressful meant that it was more useful to focus on what happened when an individual feels stressed. A third later theme was an increasing emphasis on positive well-being, as opposed to simply removing a negative feeling of being stressed.

Some useful general books about stress

Visit the health and well-being section of any good bookshop and you will find a wide range of books dealing with stress. It would be a good idea to browse them since authors take very different approaches to stress and some approaches may suit you more than others. We've selected a few which you should find both informative and readable.

Why Zebras Don't Get Ulcers by Robert M. Sapolsky (St Martin's Press, 2004) has an emphasis on physiological responses to stressful situations.

How to Deal With Stress by Stephen Palmer and Cary Cooper (Kogan Page, 2007) is a practical, readable approach by two respected writers in the field.

Counselling for Stress Problems by Stephen Palmer and Windy Dryden (Sage, 1994) is written for counsellors, and provides a more in-depth approach. Sometimes it's helpful to imagine you are your own counsellor.

Some more specialised texts on stress

If you are interested in the theoretical issues around stress, its definition and how it is seen in relation to people's working environment, these are some classic academic texts which are good starting points to the literature.

Background texts

Cary Cooper and Philip Dewe have written *Stress: A Brief History* (Blackwell, 2004). This is an accessible exploration of the development of ideas about stress – a good starting point for anyone interested in the theoretical aspects.

Hans Selye's book *The Stress of Life* (McGraw Hill, 1978) is a classic text.

Models of stress

Rob Briner and Shirley Reynolds have questioned the prevalent model of stress in their 1993 paper 'Bad theory and bad practice in occupational stress' (*The Occupational Psychologist*, 19, 8–13) and in their chapter in Stephen Palmer and Windy Dryden's book *Stress Management and Counselling: Theory, Practice, Research and Methodology* (Cassell, 1996).

A review of models of stress can be found in the paper entitled; 'Models of stress in organizational research: a metatheoretical perspective' by J.A. Weekley, J.R. Eulberg and R.S. Bhagat in the journal *Human Relations* (1988).

Life events

The well-known Holmes–Rahe scale for assessing the impact of life events is described in the 1967 paper 'The social readjustment rating scale' by T.H. Holmes and R.H. Rahe (*Journal of Psychosomatic Research*, 11, 213–218).

Sometimes, continual minor stressful events can be as damaging as major life events; the 1988 paper by A. DeLongis, S. Folkman and R.S. Lazarus on 'The impact of daily stress on health and mood: psychological and social resources as mediators' (*Journal of Personality and Social Psychology*, 54(3), 486–495) explores this issue.

2

Ways of handling stress and anxiety

(or, What can I do about the stuff that life is throwing at me?)

Emergency help for immediate stress. General methods for handling stress. Ways of preventing stress. Ways of achieving well-being.

This chapter begins with emergency help for immediate, urgent stressors. The following sections then give suggestions for getting less urgent stressors under control. After that, we deal with ways of preventing or reducing common stressors; finally, we discuss ways of achieving positive well-being, and moving your life towards where you want to be. There are further techniques, tips and exercises in the appendices, which you might find useful if you're in the middle of a stressful situation.

EMERGENCY HELP FOR IMMEDIATE STRESSES

The following sections give quick stopgap support for the following problems:

- panic attacks
- serious injury or crime
- serious bad news
- feeling that your life has fallen apart.

The sections after these give more in-depth information and techniques for handling stressors when the situation is less urgent.

Are you having a panic attack – feeling terrified, faint, with shallow breathing and clammy skin?

If so:

- sit down – if there's no chair, sit on the floor
- breathe in slowly, counting slowly to four

- hold your breath, counting slowly to four
- breathe out slowly, counting slowly to four
- hold your breath, counting slowly to four
- repeat.

This should get your carbon dioxide levels back to normal within a minute or thereabouts, and clear away the feeling of panic. Panic attacks feel horrible when they strike, but there are effective ways of handling them, such as the one above. Sitting down is helpful in terms of blood pressure, but is also useful because it reduces the risk of damage through bumping your head if you do faint. Some sufferers worry about whether or not they'll die during an attack. What actually happens is that if you faint your brain stops thinking about whatever was making you panic in the first place and then normal physiology takes over; you'll wake up again in a few seconds.

How does this strategy work? The usual way to handle panic attacks is to get your physiology stabilised, in particular your blood pressure and your carbon dioxide levels. During panic attacks, people hyperventilate, which drives down their carbon dioxide levels and gives rise to the light-headed feeling. One simple way of fixing this is to breathe into a paper bag (or your cupped hands if you don't have a bag); the bag will store the carbon dioxide from your exhalation, and after a few breaths your carbon dioxide levels will be back to normal. Another simple way of handling panic attacks is to use breathing exercises, such as the one above. These exercises do two things: they (a) occupy the brain with something other than the thing it was panicking about and (b) get your physiology into a more normal state as regards blood pressure and carbon dioxide levels.

Once you've stopped the panic attack, you should talk to a supportive friend or counsellor about it. If it was triggered by an underlying anxiety or phobia, then your life will be improved by fixing the underlying cause. Most people find reasons to avoid doing this, because of an understandable worry that the treatment will be almost as bad as the panic attack; in fact, the treatments usually involve calm relaxation, and can be actively pleasant.

Is there blood involved?

This is a vivid, memorable figure of speech referring to whether or not physical injury has occurred. If either you or someone else has been injured, raped, or otherwise traumatised, then:

- Stabilise the immediate situation (get yourself or the person involved into a safe place and stop any serious bleeding).
- If you're starting to panic, breathe slowly and deeply, counting slowly to four on each breath, and pausing for a few seconds between breaths.

- Call for proper help – if in doubt, call 999 and explain the situation to the operator.
- If you are feeling physically shocked (cold, shaky, faint, dizzy or can't think clearly) keep yourself warm, eat or drink something sweet to raise your blood sugar levels, and find someone to be with you.

Err on the side of safety; the 999 operators are trained to deal with stressed callers, and will advise you on which service is needed. For instance, if a friend has had a fall, and is dazed and bleeding from the ears, then you might not be sure whether to call for an ambulance or to drive them to A&E (Accident and Emergency) at the local hospital. Other useful emergency contacts include NHS Direct, the local police station and your university 24-hour counselling service. There are other contacts you may find helpful, and we have provided a list for you to complete in Appendix 2. Their numbers are easily found via directory enquiries, but since most of these numbers are local, it's not possible for us to list them here. If in doubt, it's always better to err on the side of calling 999 than to risk having someone die because you were afraid to bother the emergency services.

Once the crisis is over, and you are ready to think about what to do next, you can read through Chapter 6 on life events

Have you had serious bad news?
If so:

- Take some slow, deep breaths to help you stay calm and sensible.
- Decide whether you have to do anything immediately (like in the next two minutes). Usually you don't – generally another five minutes won't make any difference to the bad news, but will give you more time to think about what's best to do.
- If you do have to do something immediately, then do it. If it's not immediately obvious what requires doing, then your best option is to take a few minutes to think through the situation calmly and clearly.
- If you don't have to do anything immediately, then turn to Chapter 6, which contains advice about classic major life events and what to do about them.
- Call a capable friend and ask them to be available for backup – emotional support, notifying the department and feeding the cat if you need to go home suddenly, and so on.
- If the bad news involves a life event such as a family member being seriously ill, then read Chapter 6 on life events when you get a spare moment.
- If the bad news involves yourself, such as bad exam results, then read the section below about when your life feels as if it's falling apart.

Sometimes people get delayed shock after bad news – they're numbed at the time, and it's only hours or days later that the full emotional impact hits them. If this happens, and you find yourself panicking, treat it as a panic attack (see first section above). If it strikes while you are driving (for example, on your way to a sick relative after hearing the news), then pull over in the first safe place and wait until you're sure you've sorted out the panic before even thinking about going anywhere. If you realise you're not in a fit state to drive, then you can try calling the AA/RAC/a friend/a taxi to get you to somewhere safe.

It's also quite normal after hearing bad news to become obsessively focused on some minor issue, such as whether you'll inherit that nice vase of Aunt Kate's if she dies. This can leave you wondering afterwards whether you're a callous monster deep down, but that isn't the case; what happens is that the mind often tries to block out unwelcome major issues by focusing on minor ones instead. The minor issue often involves something practical, like arrangements for getting an essay handed in. It's very helpful to have an efficient friend around at such times, to steer you gently away from the minor issues and to help you do what's needed for the major ones.

Are you feeling that your life has fallen apart, and you don't know how to start fixing it?

- If you're feeling distraught and unstable, with nobody to turn to, then call the university's 24-hour counselling service.
- Don't make any impulsive decisions that you might regret later, such as withdrawing from your course.
- If you can't face calling the 24-hour counselling service, then take some slow, deep breaths, and read the more detailed section on page 18, about handling feelings of being out of control.

HANDLING STRESS

This section goes into more detail about techniques for handling stress, and about how these techniques work.

Relaxation and centring techniques

One set of techniques deals with feelings of panic and anxiety; these are usually referred to as relaxation or centring techniques. The term 'centring' is a reference to the image of getting yourself back into balance, centred around the real inner you, as opposed to focused on ephemeral external issues. Centring techniques are usually based around a core of shared features. One feature is removing external distractors – being somewhere quiet, without passers-by or ringing phones. Another is slow, regular breathing, which helps induce the relaxation response, a physiological state where the pulse rate slows, blood pressure drops and the brainwaves shift into the characteristic patterns of relaxation; it usually takes about five to twenty minutes to reach this state. A third is the use of music, soothing sounds or mental images to focus the mind on something other than the preoccupations and hassles of daily life. We've included a variety of these techniques in the appendices. They're closely related to meditation, though that is often linked to a set of beliefs, rather than being based solely on physiology.

You can use these techniques as part of your daily life; twenty minutes of relaxation each day can be very effective for keeping things in perspective, and helping you to feel balanced and well. You can also use them when occasion arises, such as if you're experiencing exam nerves (with the obvious proviso that you shouldn't use them in contexts like driving a car, where you need to be fully alert). The same techniques are widely used to tackle various aspects of stress, including phobias, anxiety, exam nerves, obsessive and intrusive thoughts, and feeling generally out of control. A widely used way of tackling these problems is to use a relaxation technique until you're feeling completely calm, and then to imagine a very mild form of whatever you're worried about – for instance, child's drawing of a very small spider, in the distance, if you're phobic about spiders (see Chapter 1). You keep using the relaxation technique while you imagine this, and thereby learn to associate the image with a feeling of calm. Once you're completely comfortable with the very mild image, you can then move on to the next stage, and so on until you're comfortable with the whole range. It's best to do this with a professional, who'll help you to stay calm and relaxed. It's usually fast (two or three one-hour sessions) and very comfortable.

Case study, from Susie: Joe's fear of lifts was a real pain to him. Merely thinking about getting into one set off a train of unhelpful, panicky feelings. First, he learned to deeply and quickly relax. Then he constructed a hierarchy of possible situations concerning lifts, from watching people going in and out of lifts, to being stuck in a lift, between floors. Whilst he was very relaxed, he was asked to imagine each situation in turn, until, several sessions later, he could imagine even the most stressful without feeling anxious. The next step was to test his new confidence out in reality. We went into shops with large lifts, watched people using them, got in and rode up first one floor, then two and so on. All the time he was reminded to practise relaxation. After about an hour of lifts, we

(Continued)

progressed to a tiny lift in a tower block. Part of the therapy was to make going in lifts a boring, dull pastime rather than something to be feared. Joe also agreed that being stuck in a lift was a low probability event that he need not concern himself with thoughts of. Now he was so good at relaxing that he knew he would cope with that situation if it ever arose.

These techniques are very effective for relieving the immediate feelings of stress. For the underlying causes of those feelings, there are other techniques and approaches. These range from the very practical (for example, life-planning using lists and prioritised goals) to the intangible (for example, psychotherapy); within a single approach, different professionals may vary widely in their favoured methods. Which is best? That's a reasonable question; the answer will depend on what you are like, what your problems are like, and what the professional is like. Often, the immediate problem is actually a side-effect of a very different underlying problem, which only becomes apparent when you've been working with a professional for a while.

There are other issues to take into account. One is where the line should be drawn between personal choice and a problem needing to be fixed. For instance, some people with bipolar disorder (formerly known as manic depressives) are extremely creative when in the manic phase, and view the bleak horrors of the depressive phase as being a price they're willing to pay for the creativity; for such people, their condition is a gift with a price attached, not a straightforward problem to be fixed. It's easy to make the judgement for cases at each end of the spectrum, but cases in the middle are not so easy. A related issue is that counselling and psychotherapy are like swimming across a pond – the swimming can stir up a lot of mud that's been lying beneath the surface, and there's a decision to make about whether the journey across the pond is worth the stirring up of the mud. Sometimes the answer is yes; a wise psychotherapist can help you work through unresolved problems that might otherwise have cast a blighting shadow across the rest of your life. Other times the answer is no; there's considerable debate among professionals about when it's best to let minor issues lie undisturbed to wither away with time, rather than turning them into a major issue by bringing them to the forefront of your mind. It's a difficult, grey area. As a very rough rule of thumb, if you feel uneasy about a counsellor, or you feel that they're pushing a personal agenda, particularly one that involves fostering negative feelings towards an individual or a group of individuals, then you should consider changing to someone else.

> *Case study, from Susie:* Clare came to see me once a week throughout her academic course. The sessions always took the same form. She would arrive carrying two bags of shopping. This was dumped on the floor and she stood between the bags and started to talk. She never sat down and never stopped talking. For fifty minutes. At the end of the time she would ask, 'Is the same time next week OK?' I would say 'Yes. See you then,' and she would leave. I had barely spoken for the whole of the time but I understood, from what she was saying, that she was sorting out her life. By chance, I was introduced to her father. 'So glad to meet you,' he said. 'My daughter Clare thinks you are wonderful!' Sometimes, a sympathetic listener can act as a safety valve, reduce pressure and help you to resolve the issues that are making you stressed, just by listening.

If you feel that you are faced with problems or feelings that you cannot deal with alone, we strongly advise that you seek professional help from a qualified counsellor or psychotherapist. That said, you may feel that you are in a position to address some of the feelings of stress yourself. So, what can you do about the underlying causes of stress? A lot of these involve feeling that your life is unstructured, out of control, unpredictable, unpleasant and generally a mess, so we've approached this area from the viewpoint of getting your life back under control.

Handling addictive behaviour

We usually associate addictive behaviour with dangerous or illegal activities, such as gambling, alcoholism or drug abuse. But all sorts of behaviour can become addictive, and any addiction is going to raise your stress levels because, by definition, you are not going to be in control of your life. When we are feeling stressed, depressed or anxious, it's a signal to the brain that something is wrong; and the brain will look for a quick fix to get its physiology back to normal. The quick fix may be in the form of sex, drugs or rock 'n' roll, or nicotine, alcohol, eating, shopping, computer gaming, weight-lifting or all-night clubbing. What happens is that the quick fix will give you a high which makes you feel better for a while – and then you come down from the high, find your problems haven't gone away, and that the quick fix may itself have made things worse. You address this by going for another quick fix, which makes the situation even more difficult and so on. Strategies that make your situation worse are known as *maladaptive strategies* and are best avoided if you want to stay in control of your life and away from addiction. There are a couple of ways to do this. One is to recognise that if you're feeling low, your brain needs a 'high' to balance itself. The art is in choosing a 'high' that has positive benefits, or at least no serious downside. This is why some people are such strident advocates of sport and exercise, which can give you a great feeling of well-being, and keep you fit into the bargain. The problem is that even activities which do you good – like sport – or no harm – like playing computer games – can themselves turn into a damaging addiction, with high costs in terms of time, money and stress levels. One way to avoid this happening is to have a range of strategies available for when you need a quick fix to make you feel better, not just one or two. Use them in turn. So Monday's quick fix might be a brisk walk, Tuesday's lying down with your eyes closed listening to a favourite album, Wednesday's playing squash, Thursday's watching a DVD, Friday's going out for a drink, and so on.

Another strategy is to employ *delayed gratification*. Babies find delayed gratification impossible because of their immature brains. They want something, and they want it now. You will doubtless be able to think of some adult acquaintances who have the same problem. Let's say you are struggling with your academic course, avoid tackling the problems and make yourself feel better by having a few pints in the union bar each evening. You do not have a 'drink problem' as such, but your expenditure on alcohol is escalating, your assignments are stacking up, you feel permanently sluggish and you are putting on weight. If you decide to deal with the problem by never darkening the doors of the union bar again, you will simply make yourself feel worse. A more effective solution would be to decide to stay in on a Monday evening, say, and get some work done. The following week, stay in on a Monday and Tuesday. The week after, make it Monday, Tuesday and Thursday. If this seems too drastic, try delaying your visit to the bar for an hour, then two hours, then three, to cut down on available drinking time. If you are still finding this difficult, you may have a drink problem, or at least a self-control problem, so seek professional help. The advice you get on controlling one form of addictive behaviour will probably prove very useful if you overcome one kind of addiction only to develop another as soon as you find the stress levels rising.

Handling the feeling of being out of control

Panic attacks are what the medical profession calls 'acute' as opposed to 'chronic.' These terms are used differently in the medical world from in everyday life, which is a fine source of potential confusion when medics interact with non-medics. 'Acute' in medical language means that something happens at a particular point in time; 'chronic' in medical language means that it goes on for an extended length of time. Stress often arises out of a situation that appears set to go on for a long time or for the foreseeable future – that's generally what makes the situation stressful, if you aren't sure that you can keep going till the end, or aren't sure if there even is an end to it. That in turn is usually bound up closely with a feeling of being out of control. As a general principle, anything that helps you feel you're getting your life under control is likely to help reduce stress. Fortunately, there are usually plenty of things you can do to help yourself with this. Three useful starting points are:

- look at the bigger picture
- have a temporary working plan
- start small and work up.

Looking at the bigger picture

A striking feature of stress and related concepts is that they involve a lot of obsessive thoughts, typically miserable ones, which usually lead to getting things completely out of proportion. Here are some examples.

Embarrassment: a !angled web

The great Joe Haldeman wrote a science fiction story called *A !angled Web*, about an alien species called the !ang (the exclamation mark stands for a clicking sound, but that's another story). They had a richly formalised way of handling embarrassment. The embarrassed person would begin by saying 'I am embarrassed.' They would then elaborate on the extent and the consequences of the embarrassment, with the phrasing being different every time – for instance, 'My cheeks grow hot with embarrassment. They grow so hot that the sea dries up. They grow so hot that the land dries up. The fish die, the plants die, the animals die.' They would then conclude by saying 'All die. I am embarrassed.' Embarrassment isn't much fun, but if fear of embarrassment is holding you back from doing something, then it's worth considering whether you're weaving a !angled web for yourself and getting things just a bit out of proportion.

Brooding fantasies of failure; the dog on the string

When worried, it's traditional to brood about the problem and spin elaborate fantasies of gloom and despair. For instance, you might find yourself imagining a disastrous failure in your next exam, dragging down your degree to a level where nobody is willing to employ you, so you end up begging in the street, with a dog on a string, and eventually die of hypothermia, abandoned by the dog and miserable and starving. Well, yes, it could conceivably happen, but it's not the usual outcome of a bad mark in an exam by any stretch of the imagination. Planning for reasonable worst-case scenarios is sensible; weaving elaborate fantasies of failure isn't. The time spent on a miserable fantasy can be spent instead on one about being happy; better for you, and more pleasant.

HEAL – assessing thoughts, so you can replace bad ones with good ones

You can assess a thought in terms of its:

Helpfulness – is it helping you in any way?
Evidence – is there good evidence to support it?
Accuracy – does it correspond reasonably well to reality?
Logic – does it make sense?

So, for instance, the thought 'I'm going to fail this exam' is unlikely to be helping you. If you've passed all your previous exams, and this exam isn't significantly different from them, then the thought isn't based on good evidence. Sometimes a thought does have some evidence behind it, but doesn't match well with reality – for instance, the thought 'those lecturers stopped talking when I went past, so they must have been talking about me' has some evidence (if they really did stop talking) but is unlikely to be accurate; it's much more likely that they stopped talking for some other reason, like having reached a break in the conversation. The dividing line between evidence, accuracy and logic can be fuzzy, but that's not terribly important; what matters is the concept of checking whether a particular thought is doing you good and is related reasonably closely to reality.

When you're stressed, thoughts tend to go round in your head like a hyperactive hamster in an over-oiled wheel. Simply trying to throw a thought out isn't usually effective; the very action of trying to throw it out involves thinking about it, which gets you back to where you started from. What works much better is replacing that thought with something else, particularly something that is going somewhere. A prominent feature of stress is the feeling of no escape – going round a set of thoughts endlessly because you can't see a way out of them. The more you go round, the more of your attention they take up; it's a vicious cycle. One handy metaphor is that a vicious cycle of this sort is like a runaway riderless motorbike on a wall of death circuit; it's going round in circles, and you may not be able to stop it right now, but that doesn't mean that you need to jump on top of it and try to bring it to a halt. What you can do instead is leave it to run out of petrol and grind to a halt, while you get on with something completely different, in the form of positive thoughts.

The positive thoughts you choose should be helpful, rational and reasonably close to reality. For example, if you're worried about just getting through the exams, you can remind yourself that they won't go on for ever, and that you're going to treat yourself to a really enjoyable day out to reward yourself for doing them all, regardless of how well you did. You can imagine the taste of that rich chocolate biscuit as you sit watching people go by, and the smell of the freshly made coffee in its white china cup on the table in front of you. It's helpful, because it's moving you into a positive cycle, and it's rational and reasonably close to reality, because all it requires is the cost of a coffee and biscuit. It's also giving you positive reinforcement about your ability to get through the exams.

If you're going through testing times, you're likely to feel physically tense, probably without realising it. The physical tension will tire you, so it's a good idea to do some muscle-relaxing exercises periodically. The one below has the added advantage of being good for when you've spent too long at the keyboard or hunched over a book – common problems for students. (It's more productive, and ergonomically sound, to take a ten minute break every hour when studying.)

If you're feeling tense and sore around the shoulders:

- Straighten up in your chair and close your eyes.
- Take several deep breaths and concentrate on your breathing.
- Breathe in and lift your shoulders as high as you can.
- Hold your shoulders high while you take three slow breaths.
- Breathe gently out while you drop your shoulders as low as possible.
- Keep your shoulders dropped for one breath.

Repeat the exercise three times.

Having a temporary working plan

If you're feeling that your life is out of control, then having a plan will get some of it under control. A temporary plan will buy you enough time to put together something more sophisticated and far-reaching. Here's an example of a temporary working plan, with explanations for each part.

- Get to bed by 11.00 am and up by 7.30 am throughout this week. (Lack of sleep causes stress, and makes small stressors appear much bigger than they really are.)
- Spend twenty minutes on Tuesday and Thursday evening doing centring exercises. (These will help you stay calm.)
- Arrange a meeting with an approachable lecturer to discuss ways forward with your academic work. (This will help you identify possible solutions that you hadn't known about before. It can also help you find out about other support services, such as support with essay-writing technique.)
- Have an evening out with friends on Wednesday. (This is fun, and helps maintain your social support.)
- Spend twenty minutes on Friday morning planning the weekend and what you'll do next week. (This saves you from a potentially bleak unstructured weekend, and helps you move on to a better plan.)

This isn't the world's most sophisticated strategy, but it's a start. You'll probably have already spotted some obvious gaps in it; this is a good sign, because it means that you're starting to move forward and work out better ways of getting things done.

Starting small, and working up

Another easy but effective approach to tackling stress is to develop small, safe routines – things that you do at the same time each day or each week, or in the same way. For instance, you might start your day by having a cup of coffee while you get your working materials into place, easing yourself gently into working mode. Similarly, you can do your shopping at the same time every week, and have a standard set of favourite meals for some days of the week, or a standard 'emergency meal' for when you can't face making another decision about what to eat. Each of these routines means one less thing that you have to make decisions about. End-of-day routines are at least as important as start-of-day ones; they help you to approach sleep with calm, positive feelings, so that you're more likely to wake up refreshed the next day. Don't allow routines or rituals to dominate your life. Having a 'lucky T-shirt' that you wear to exams is fine; wearing it every day and refusing to wash it, in case you wash away the luck, is obsessive (and smelly). The routines should be helpful servants, not dominating masters.

A related strategy is to tackle small manageable tasks. You can keep a list of these pinned up somewhere visible, or in a frequently used folder. They're things like tidying up your desktop, mucking out a bag, or cleaning the sink. Being small and manageable, these tasks don't take long, they're useful, they'll make your life a bit better, they're evidence that you have control over some of your world, and they also help break you out of cycles of negative thoughts. Small manageable tasks make excellent displacement activities – the things you do when you're putting off something that you find unpleasant. For instance, if you're putting off writing a difficult letter, then instead of displacing by watching television, you could displace by tidying your desk – it gives you the opportunity to gear yourself up to facing the difficult task, time to think about it, and gives you a tidy desk.

A variant on this theme is to have small manageable goals, either as goals in their own right, or as part of some longer-term strategy. For example, if you're saving money to pay off a debt, or to fund your holiday in the Bahamas, you can choose to stay in and read a book one evening rather than going out, and squirrel away the amount of money that you'd otherwise have spent on nightlife. This makes staying at home into a positive choice, and you can schedule in a reward for yourself, such as a sticky bun and cocoa mid-evening. The goals need to be clear and achievable – 'clean the kitchen windowsill' is better than 'do some cleaning.' This leads into the next section, which describes ways of preventing stressors from arising in the first place, and ways of preparing for any stresses that can't be prevented.

PREVENTION AND PREPARATION

An effective strategy is to prevent the bad things that you can reasonably prevent, and to prepare for those that you can't. It's wise to get the balance right – you'll eventually reach the *point of diminishing returns*, after which any extra effort doesn't make much more difference. Spending some of your time preventing bad things is sensible; spending all of your time making contingency plans for increasingly remote possibilities is not good for you, and is not a good use of time.

Getting started

Getting started can be the hardest part, especially with tasks that look unpleasant, boring and/or threatening. However, unwelcoming tasks seldom curl up and die if left alone, so it's better to get going with them. Three good ways of getting started are the salami technique, the Mars bar technique and the BANJO technique, described below.

The salami technique involves the difference between trying to eat a whole salami in one go, which is not advisable, and trying to eat the same salami cut into thin slices, presented in several different ways in several meals, which is much more appealing. If you have a large chunk of work that you are putting off, divide it into small ten to twenty minute sections and do one at a time. It then appears much less off-putting and when you do one section, you may find it is easy to do a second immediately after it. Even doing one section at a time will soon build up to a sizeable chunk of the project, making it easier to tackle as the deadline draws near. (This approach is sometimes phrased as a joke: 'Q: How would you eat an elephant? A: One bite at a time.')

The Mars bar technique involves actual food rather than allegorical food. It consists of delaying any sort of reward until you have actually done a chunk of work. Sit down, start, continue working, no coffee, no chat, no TV, complete the planned chunk of work, and then give yourself the Mars bar (or equivalent). Only good behaviour gets the reward. This does need self-discipline initially, but it's very productive once you get into the habit.

The BANJO technique is named after the acronym for 'Bang A Nasty Job Off.' Undone nasty jobs are like the monster in the cupboard in horror movies; they don't go away, and the more you think about them, the worse they seem. When you get them out of the cupboard, though, they soon start looking like someone in a rubber suit. It's the same with festering undone jobs; the sooner you do them, the sooner they stop haunting you and making you feel bad. If you have a nasty job to do, do it as soon as possible: many BANJO players do their unpleasant jobs first thing in the working day, so that the rest of the day feels horror-free and enjoyable. If it was a particularly important task, you could give yourself a reward as a further pat on your back.

Lifestyle and well-being

One of the tricky features about giving advice is that the advice may be helpful, but so well established that it can sound like a self-evident cliché – for example, that people should get plenty of exercise and sleep. In such instances, we've borrowed the semi-ironic term 'a Good Thing' from the humorous history book *1066 and All That* as an indication that the advice is sound, but also as an indication that we can sympathise with readers who had heard the same advice more than often enough before opening this book.

A lot of stress-related bad feelings involve the interaction between the body and the mind. When you're stressed, anxious or depressed, it's easy to neglect your body, which leads to physiological reactions that make you feel even worse. Some simple ways to counter this are described below.

Exercise is a Good Thing; it stimulates the body to release endorphins, which make you feel better, as well as having assorted other positive effects. The exercise doesn't need to involve jogging outfits or gyms occupied by scarily muscled people; twenty minutes of walking per day is enough to make a difference. In the winter, it's a good idea to get some daylight, and a brisk walk at a bright time of day will help you feel better and sleep better. If this sounds a bit boring to you, then you can set yourself a small manageable goal of making the exercise fun in some way and fitting it into your schedule.

Getting enough sleep is a Good Thing. People usually sleep best by having a regular bedtime, a regular bedtime routine, and a calm sleeping environment. The bed should be reserved for getting to sleep (reading, or thinking calm thoughts), for sleeping and for sex – not for eating, watching TV, arguing, writing essays, or the like. The bed needs to have associations of calm, of post-coital snuggling, and of sleep.

Watch the caffeine levels. Due to some lamentable fault in the design of the universe, caffeine doesn't help you sleep well, and is found in tea, coffee, many fizzy drinks and chocolate (to add insult to injury, the better the chocolate, the higher the caffeine dose). If you're having trouble sleeping, then try not having caffeine during the hours before bedtime.

Watch the alcohol levels. Alcohol in moderate doses can take the edge off your worries, and social drinking can be very enjoyable, but in large doses alcohol will add more worries, while leaving the original worries still in place when you sober up. Alcohol plays a large part in student life, and many students feel that if they don't drink heavily then they'll look bad in front of their mates. It's worth turning that problem round, and asking yourself whether it's really a good idea to hang around with people who want you to do something that's bad for you.

Healthy diet is another Good Thing. This is not the same as living on lettuce and broccoli, nor is it the same as spending hours at the stove. There are plenty of good cookbooks from which you can learn to produce fast, cheap, meals; we have a section on the essentials of eating elsewhere in this book.

Have a life. Friends and a support network are important, and so is having another facet or two in your life apart from studying and the Student Union. Having several strands in your life will help keep each strand in perspective, so you don't get so worked up about things. As usual, you need to keep a sense of perspective – having several varied activities in your life is good, but having dozens will over-stretch you and cause more problems. The different activities don't need to be anything major, like international competitive hockey; just going to the cinema once a month with some friends can be enough to keep you in touch with other people, and give you something to think about apart from exams.

Handling uncertainty and decision-making

A common feature in stress is uncertainty. This can often be handled by simply getting the relevant information; it can also be reduced by having a plan for each of the outcomes that may emerge. It's particularly useful to have a worst-case plan which is positive, rather than involving sitting miserably in a corner waiting for death. For instance, if the worst case is that you end up unemployed for a year, you can develop a plan for using that time to do things that you wouldn't otherwise have time to do, like practising your calligraphy or learning a new skill or making new friends. One common source of uncertainty involves agonising about whether or not you've made the right decision; we talk about handling obsessive thoughts in a later section. Meanwhile, here are some useful ways of handling decisions.

Work backwards from where you want to be

This includes wanting to be somewhere that keeps your options open. People often become obsessed by an intermediate goal, such as getting a highly paid job, which has all sorts of associated problems. When you look at your higher-level goals, you often see a much better way of getting to them than the problematic intermediate goal. For instance, if you want a highly paid job so that you can afford to travel, then you might instead consider simply getting a job that involves a lot of travel.

Identify the possible options and relevant factors

What are the possible options, and what are the preconditions for each option? There are usually more options than you realise; it's worth doing some background research if the decision is an important one.

Check the question

If you can't answer a question, this may be because you're asking the wrong question; subtly changing it could make a lot of difference. One way is to imagine the possible answers to the question; if they're either silly or impossible to know, then it's not the most useful of questions. For example, asking 'Will I be happy at Fenlands University?' doesn't do too well by this criterion, since that's impossible to know in advance; asking 'Would going to Fenlands University be easily compatible with my love of rock climbing?' performs much better.

Remove irrelevant distractors

This simply involves crossing out any options that are out of the question for whatever reason, and identifying the options that are definite contenders.

Choose the best contender

What does 'best' mean? That depends. Think about one of the worst contenders. What makes it bad? That tells you at least one criterion that you can flip around to assess what constitutes a good option. Other things worth considering are whether an option is irreversible (it's usually better to go for reversible ones if possible) and what the payoffs look like. The payoffs in this context are the possible outcomes from an option; some options may pay off spectacularly if all goes well, but have disastrous consequences if things go wrong, whereas others won't pay off so spectacularly in a best case, but won't cause significant problems in a worst case.

Flip a coin

If you can't decide between two options, then this probably means that they're both equally good, so choose one at random and get on with your life.

TIMETABLING AND PLANNING

Timetabling and planning are very effective ways of getting pleasure and calm into your life; something as simple as scheduling Wednesday 2–3 pm for relaxation will give you an hour that's there just for that purpose. They also help you to spend your time more effectively. There's an effect called a *Pareto distribution*, in which 20 per cent of one thing gives you 80 per cent of another thing. For instance, 20 per cent of the time you spend on an essay will typically produce 80 per cent of the text – the remaining 20 per cent of the text will be fiddly bits that take 80 per cent of the time. If you're stressed because of lack of time, then it's a good idea to look critically at the most time-consuming activities in your life, and to see whether you're spending time on them beyond the point of diminishing returns. Instead of jumping straight into the essay and working for ten frenzied hours, for instance, you'll usually be better off spending half an hour planning the essay, then working in a more focused way for five or six hours. That gives you as good a mark, but with a lot less stress and a lot more free time to spend on other things. What other things should you spend your time on? It's your life, so it's your choice. Things that make you happy, as long as they're not damaging someone else, are usually a good choice.

How to decide how you spend your time

An important starting point is to clarify your goals. If you have a clear idea of what you want out of life, your goals are obvious. People who have clearly worked-out goals can withstand a lot of stress because they keep the goal in sight. Suppose you want to pursue your interest in mazes (or motor racing, or whatever else your hobby may be). That is too vague to be a goal. You need to refine it so that it is SMART: Specific, Measurable, Achievable, Realistic and Time-limited. Making it *Specific* could be 'To visit the most interesting mazes in Europe'; *Measurable* would be identifying which those were, and listing them. To make sure this was *Achievable* you'd need to work out whether there were any practical blockers, such as one of those mazes being in the middle of a long-running war zone. *Realistic* involves assessing whether it's actually sensible and worth trying, as opposed to possible in theory. You might in principle be able to visit each of them by travelling non-stop through a weekend, but it would be more realistic to visit them in a specified vacation, or after you graduate. You also need a specific *Time-limitation*, such as 'Next year' or 'By the time I'm 30.' This will help ensure that you actually get round to doing it, and will also help you set intermediate goals, such as applying for a passport or booking a ticket for the relevant date. Having clear goals lets you work out what is important to you. Anything that moves you closer to your goals is something that counts as important. If one of your goals is to laugh a lot, then watching comedy on TV becomes more important and watching the news becomes less important. Spend time on things that are important to you, and you will be less stressed. It also helps to work out what you would do if you met obstacles along the way to your goal. You can brainstorm possible setbacks, then think about how you would get round them. You will then be prepared for most eventualities and have plan B (and C) in place. If you wait until there is a crisis, you will have to decide what to do whilst under pressure, which is seldom fun and which rarely leads to good decisions. It's better to make the contingency plans in advance, when you are calm and have plenty of time.

Using reminders and lists

It's a good idea to write reminders to yourself to nudge you back into positive thoughts if you drift out of them. You can write a big version to put in your personal space, to remind you of just what the good thought was; you can then use something associated with this in shared space, to spare you potential embarrassment if you're shy. For example, if you're in a shared house you can put a little blue sticky dot next to the kettle and another on the bathroom mirror, and tell your housemates that it's to remind you about exam preparation; each time you see one of those dots, it's actually a reminder to you about your positive thought. Lists are indispensable, but not just any old list will do. Prioritise everything on the list and do the most important things first. Only move on to the less important things when you have made real progress on the top priority tasks. Or, if a top priority job gets too hard or too boring, use a low priority task as a 'filler.' Avoid doing several low priority, trivial tasks and letting them fill a morning. You may feel smug at having crossed six things off your list, but you won't have achieved anything worthwhile. When you have crossed all the things you have done off your list, you will be left with a rather depressing list of the things you didn't do. Making a list of things you *have* done is a good way to realise that you have achieved lots and will boost your mood.

Getting on with your life – forget the fart, and put down the supermodel

Most people worry occasionally about the risk of doing something silly which will haunt them for the rest of their lives. There's a classic story, often re-told, of a noble at the court of Elizabeth I who, when bowing to the great queen, accidentally let fly with a very loud fart. He fled the court in embarrassment, and lived quietly in the provinces for twenty years, eventually returning to the court just after the defeat of the Spanish armada, when he thought that recent events would have driven memories of his *faux pas* far from everyone's mind. The queen greeted him warmly, with the immortal line 'How pleased we are to see you again; we had quite forgotten the fart.' A good story, but an almost identical one is also told about a noble at the court of one of the great Islamic caliphs, raising the suspicion that it might be no more than a richly documented urban legend.

So what do you do about it? There's a Zen story about two monks who meet a beautiful woman at a flooded river; she can't wade across without spoiling her expensive clothes. One monk offers to carry her across; she accepts, he does so, and they go their separate ways. After a couple of miles in monastic silence the second monk says to the first monk, 'That's outrageous! We're not even supposed to talk to women, but you carried that one right across the river!' The first monk replies, 'Are you still carrying the woman? I set her down two miles ago.' (All right, so she wasn't a supermodel, but why spoil a memorable and useful good principle for the sake of pedantry?) We all make mistakes sometimes; we need to learn from them, then set down the supermodel and move on.

WELL-BEING

Fixing stress is a Good Thing, but there's more to life than that. The next section is about strategies that can help to make your life positively enjoyable and about achieving well-being.

Working backwards

When you're working out where you want to go with your life, it's tempting to focus on what's immediately in front of you, usually in the form of the option that is most familiar/easy/unthreatening. That's understandable, but it tends to nudge you gently into a gradually deeper rut, until one day you realise that there's hardly anything in your life that you like. That's a bit like choosing your holiday destination by going to the local bus station, because it's the easiest place to start, and then choosing the bus that leaves the soonest, because it involves least waiting. There's a chance that it will take you somewhere nice, but the likelihood of ending up in Corfu or Hawaii or somewhere similar is pretty slight. A better approach is to work out where you want to be, and then work backwards from that end point; if you have decided that you want to go to Hawaii, then you can start choosing the dates, flights and accommodation which will get you to that goal. It's the same with other things in your life, such as what sort of job you want, where you want to work, what you want to do with your life, and so on. This doesn't mean that your life has to be a relentless pursuit of achievements; exactly the same principle applies if you decide to lead a life of quiet monastic contemplation (in which case you'd need to find out about how to become a monk or nun, and where you can lead the said life of quiet contemplation, and so forth).

The closing scene

There's a nice scene at the end of the film *Death Becomes Her* involving the funeral eulogy for the main character. The mourners remember him fondly, as a man who gave generously to good causes and was humble despite his amazing achievements, a loyal and caring friend, a great person to talk to, and all sorts of other wonderful things. One simple but effective exercise is to think about what you would like to hear in your own eulogy – whether it would include something about what an interesting life you'd had, or what a nice person you were, or what a great parent you were, and so on. A similar exercise is to imagine yourself in old age, looking back on your life, and thinking 'I'm glad I did that.' What would the things be that you'd want to look back on? Once you've identified some of these things, you can do something about making them happen. Most of them are much more accessible than people think, particularly if they involve things that are under your control, rather than things that involve chance (such as going wreck-diving in the Bahamas, as opposed to finding a lost treasure galleon). For instance, if you want to go wreck-diving in the Bahamas, you need to do three things: save up money, sign up for a scuba diving course and book a wreck-diving holiday.

You can also do a smaller-scale version of this for events that you're concerned about. For instance, you can try imagining the interview panel for your first job reminiscing about what a wonderful interview you gave. This is a gentle way into thinking about just what would constitute a wonderful interview anyway, which will help motivate you to do some research about interview technique and about preparations for the next phase of your life. The more vivid and detailed the image, the better; you might imagine the twinkly-eyed, grey-haired woman with the glasses telling you how rare it was to meet a candidate who had done some proper background research about the organisation before applying, or the tall man saying how well you kept your cool when one of the panel members mistook you for another candidate.

Assertiveness

Many things that can cause pressure will grow if you neglect them. Putting up with a flatmate's irritating habit for months will drive you to distraction and eventually lead you to asking them to stop in an inappropriate way. If your unhygienic mate has left his smelly socks on the sofa seventeen times before you suddenly threaten to kill him if he does it again, you may get the justifiable response 'But I didn't think you minded. I've been doing it for months and you never said anything.' The time to speak up is when they have done it twice. The first time could be just a one-off, but twice is becoming a trend. (And three times is definitely enemy action.) So speak up and say it in an assertive way. Say what happened, say why that is a bad thing and request a new behaviour: 'You left your socks on the couch twice this week, and I'm upset because they make the room smell. Please keep your dirty clothes in your own room.' The last bit is important because often people can't think of anything to do to solve a problem and if you don't tell them, they will just revert to old patterns. Also, if you start a sentence with the word 'Please' it frames your request in an assertive way. If you ask assertively, and the unhelpful stuff continues, ask again. And again. And again. Each time refuse to be side-tracked, or put off. Stay calm and polite and persistent. When a flat-sharer owed rent to one of us, he wrote out the cheque seven times before he got it right. Staying calm and persistent eventually extracted the money, without lasting harm to the relationship.

Saying 'no' is sometimes difficult, especially if you don't feel you have a socially acceptable excuse. 'I don't want to' somehow seems not good enough. It helps if you offer an alternative. 'No, not tonight; how about

Wednesday?' is easier to say, and to hear. Again, be firm or you will spend your time doing things you don't want to do instead of doing the things you do want to do.

Handling criticism

Criticism can cause strain, especially if you don't know how to handle it. There are two types of criticism and you need to recognise the difference. The first is legitimate feedback that is intended to help you improve your skills. For instance, if you take a long time to come to the point in an essay and a tutor highlights a passage as irrelevant, this is constructive criticism, even though you may not feel pleased about it at the time. The other sort of criticism aims to manipulate you and make you feel bad. This type of criticism is based on a grain of truth, or the possibility – or fear – of a grain of truth.

One common response is to think that the criticism may be horribly right; another common response is to rise to the provocation by making an angry retort which shows just how much the criticism has struck home. There are much more effective ways of responding. The key principle is to refuse the emotional double-bind of either getting into an argument or of leaving the criticism unchallenged and rankling. One way of doing this is via a calmly worded response which makes it clear that you're not going to rise to the bait, but which doesn't give the critic any easy way to respond – for instance, saying 'Maybe you are right' or 'Oh, really, thanks for telling me.' The sub-text is clearly that you're confident enough not to be bothered by their opinion, and there's not much they can say to that without looking either silly or obviously aggressive. (One obvious proviso is that you shouldn't use this in response to a criticism that contradicts your basic beliefs, such as someone saying that you're a Nazi.)

Another strategy is to ask a factual question which forces the critic to come up with something tangible, such as: 'What exactly don't you like about my clothes?' This will usually either make it clear that the criticism is just a matter of subjective opinion, or, more rarely but more usefully, give you some factual information about an area where you actually could benefit from changing your ways. If you're dealing with someone who typically stores up piles of grudges, looking for an excuse to trot them out, then go for the first strategy so they don't get a chance to wheel out their list of specific complaints; if you're dealing with someone who typically says whatever comes into their head, without any thought behind it, then go for the second, so they have to back off because they don't have any specific objections to your behaviour. The best thing about this tactic is that you no longer behave like a victim, and it is such an unexpected response that it often throws your critic off balance. You may need to persist, but usually the critic just goes away and picks on someone else.

Aiming to fail often enough

If you aim to succeed in everything you do, without ever making a mistake, then that is setting you up for neurosis. If you aim to fail in everything you do, then that's setting yourself up for misery. Somewhere inbetween is healthy; what's it to be for you? If you set a sensible failure rate, then that gives you a reasonable benchmark for assessing that your overall goals are realistic. For instance, when you apply for jobs, a rejection rate of 100 per cent suggests that you're either doing something wrong or aiming too high, but an invitation-to-interview rate of 100 per cent suggests that you're aiming too low, and could go for something better. Also, aiming for a realistic achievement rate reduces the risk of becoming neurotic about success, and the risk of being guilt-racked and miserable if things don't always go as intended. You're human; every human being makes mistakes and has things go wrong sometimes; it's good to forgive others who have made mistakes and are genuinely sorry about them, so you should also forgive yourself for not being utterly perfect all the time.

SUMMARY

There are simple, effective techniques for handling the stress response; these usually involve deliberate breathing and deliberate mental imagery. There are also simple, effective techniques for sorting out your life and planning the future that you want, as part of moving on from stress towards well-being. Key themes in this include working backwards from where you want to end up; setting clear, achievable goals; re-assessing your plan at intervals, to take account of developments since the plan was made; and learning to view criticism and your own human fallibility in a positive light. This chapter dealt with general stressors. The next chapter deals with specific stressors relating to the move from school and home to university.

BIBLIOGRAPHY AND SUGGESTED FURTHER RESOURCES

Handling immediate stress

There are numerous good books on this topic; here are a few examples:

Philip Banyard's book *Applying Psychology to Health* (Hodder, 1999) is an entertaining introduction to many of the issues raised here and treats specific topics like Post-Traumatic Stress Disorder (PTSD) in more detail.

For a self-help programme to overcome PTSD, *The Trauma Trap* by David Muss (Doubleday, 1991) is a very useful practical guide.

William Dement's book *The Promise of Sleep* (Dell, 1999) is a very comprehensive coverage of the way we spend about one-third of our lives. It includes practical advice to combat failure to sleep.

The Origin of Everyday Moods by Robert Thayer (Oxford University Press, 1996) focuses on managing energy levels as well as tension and stress.

We also recommend Stafford Whiteaker's book *The Little Book of Inner Space: Your Guide to Finding Personal Peace* (Rider, 1998). This contains a lot of useful, bite-sized pieces of good advice. It's small enough to fit easily into a handbag or pocket, so if you want something calming you can carry round with you, you may find this one useful. Another good book in the same series is *The Little Book of Calm*, by P. Wilson (Penguin, 1999), which featured in the TV comedy series *Black Books*; it really does exist. If you're looking through the Little Books series, then be aware that *The Little Book of Stress* is not what it might appear from the title; it's a darkly humorous book whose front cover proclaims 'Calm is for wimps. Get real. Get stressed.'

Achieving your potential

There are many books, videos, DVDs and courses on this topic, as well as a philosophical/spiritual movement known as the Human Potential Movement.

A good, straightforward introduction to the rational-emotive approach to tackling behaviours and achieving your potential is *Peak Performance* by Windy Dryden and Jack Gordon (Management Books 2000 Ltd, 1993).

Susan Jeffers's *Feel the Fear and Do It Anyway* (Arrow Books, London, 1991 edition), is a classic book about helping yourself to make the most of your life and to achieve your dreams. It's both inspirational and realistic, as well as being very readable – the sort of book you can keep somewhere near to hand, and dip into when you need some positive thoughts, or some ideas about what you can tackle next.

Habits and behaviours

There's lots of material about curing yourself of bad habits, and getting yourself into good habits. Some of this is about low-level, specific habits such as smoking, drinking and addictive behaviour. Some is about broader issues such as your beliefs about life as a whole, and the patterns of behaviour that you use. We've listed a few books of each type.

Eric Berne's *Games People Play: The Psychology of Human Relationships* (Penguin, 1968 edition) is one of the classic books about patterns of behaviour that people use, and about how these form part of people's world-views. The mention of 'games' in the title is in some ways unfortunate, since this has connotations of leisure pastimes – Berne made the choice quite deliberately, and for good reason, but it does deter some people from reading the book. The book is clearly written, and contains numerous case studies. The main strength of the book is the identification of behaviour patterns – for instance, the 'ain't it awful?' pattern, where the person has a pattern of looking for something to complain about, and if necessary making bad things happen so that there is something about which they can complain. If you want to look at the bigger picture of how you're tackling life, then this is well worth reading.

Also by Eric Berne, *What Do You Say After You Say Hello?* (Corgi, 1996) covers similar territory to *Games People Play*, but is much more detailed.

Allen Carr's *Easy Way to Stop Smoking* (Penguin, 2006) is a good example of what to do if you have decided to stop. There is also a CD and video with the same title.

Robert Harper and Albert Ellis's book *A Guide to Rational Living* (Image Book Company, 1997) is the classic text to help you control emotion and stress by thinking more rationally.

Martin Seligman's book *Authentic Happiness: Using the New Positive Psychology to Realize Your Potential for Lasting Fulfillment* (Free Press, 2004) introduces Positive Psychology and includes practical advice to help cultivate optimism and happiness.

3

Leaving home and starting university

(or, Alone at last – rejoice or weep?)

Choosing your university and course with minimal stress. Preparing to leave home and start university. Packing, travel to university, and week zero. The first two weeks; academic, emotional and social issues to expect. Resource location and forward planning.

KNOWING WHERE YOU'RE GOING

There are plenty of sources of stress for would-be students before they even know which university they're going to. These might be well in the past by the time you read this book, but we're assuming that some readers will be given a copy by loving friends and relations while still at school, hence the inclusion of this section. Here are some classic early stressors.

- Should I be going to university in the first place?
- Which university should I go to (and does it make any difference)?
- What if I choose the wrong university?
- What if I choose the wrong course?
- What if I hate it?

We'll tackle the first question first – whether you should be going to university in the first place. Imagine that someone tells you 'Yes, you should go to university' or 'No, you shouldn't go.' Would you simply believe that? Probably not, and for good reasons; how could anyone possibly be completely sure of the answer to such a question? A better pair of starting questions would be; 'Is there any significant reason that I should not go to university?' and 'Is there any significant reason that I should go to university?' If you want a career as an architect or a doctor, for instance, then it's pretty clear that you'll need to go to university at some point. Conversely, if you've failed every exam you've sat in the last five years, then trying to go to university would probably be a bad idea. It's also worth thinking about whether university is the best route to where you want to be, and whether another type of further education might be a better choice – it's a different route, with a different goal, not a second-best for those who can't get into university. This book is written with university students in mind, but that's just for focus, not because of snobbishness about non-university routes.

If you decide that university really is what you want to do, then there's the issue of when to go. You don't have to go straight from school; many students take a gap year between school and university. There are some significant advantages in this strategy. For instance, the gap year can give you more confidence, more experience of the world, and more idea of what you want to do with your life, depending on what you do in that year; it might also allow you to save some money to help you financially through your degree, and might bring you into contact with potential employers for when you finish university, not to mention a set of friends outside your university life. If your gap year turns out to be grim, this can fill you with a steely resolve to go to university, make the most of it, and go on to something much better. For one outstanding student we know, the key motivating factor was a desire never to work again on the night shift in the local pie factory. One risk to beware involves gap years which are okay, but not very wonderful; if you're in a mediocre job, then it's easy to slip into a rut, and never quite get round to breaking out of it (for example by going to university and looking for a job which is positively enjoyable). It's possible to go to university at any point in life, not just after a gap year; many people do part-time degrees or full-time degrees when in middle age (see Chapter 10 for more about this). It's worth remembering this option if you end up with problematic exam results; if you really want to go to university, there are second chances later in life.

The next set of questions involves choice of university and choice of course. You might find it useful to work through the tips about decision-making in Chapter 2. At the end, though, you'll still probably have niggling uncertainties. It's worth bearing in mind that all British universities and courses go through a long, detailed and painstaking process of quality and control and accreditation to ensure that they're of an acceptable standard – wherever you go, whatever course you do, it will be at least good enough. Good enough for what? That's the next part of the answer; each student is likely to get different things from the same university, or the same course, or the same module or piece of coursework. One of the bleakly entertaining aspects of being a lecturer is getting student feedback forms about modules you've taught; often, the same topic gets feedback ranging from 'brilliant!' to 'a total waste of time.' It's not possible for you or anyone else to predict with certainty how you'll feel about the course that you do; so as long as you've made a reasonable decision with the information available, there's no point in agonising about it (the section on obsessive thoughts on page 19 may help if you do find yourself agonising).

What if you hate the university or the course? It's not like being in the French Foreign Legion in the old days; at university, you're allowed to change your mind. It's usually possible to change course within your university; if you hate the university, then there's no law against leaving and trying again at another university – you have the rest of your life to try again. If you're considering this route, then it's wise to start taking advice as early as possible; there's a fine balance between giving the course or university a fair trial, and leaving things till too late. Student advice services should be able to help with this. A rule of thumb that you might find useful is that if you're calmly certain that you want to leave, then that's probably the right decision; if you're not completely certain, or you're angry about something, then you should give some serious thought to staying, and fixing the situation. Finding ways of fixing a situation is a very useful skill in life, and if you can get being at university to work for you, then it gives you a richer and more interesting set of options for your life than most institutions.

BEFORE YOU START AT YOUR CHOSEN UNIVERSITY

Some of the classic stressors in the first month at university are easily preventable, if you prepare in advance.

Classic stressor	What you can do about it
I don't know how to cook	Learn basic cookery; get a basic cookery book
I don't know basic maintenance like how to wash clothes or sew on buttons	Learn and practise; get a book on basic household management
I don't know how to budget money and plan things like food shopping	Learn and practise; the book on basic household management should cover this
I don't know what to expect when I get there	Read this book's sections on the basic principles of academic life; read the university's documentation; if possible, talk to someone who's been there before
I've never been away from home before and I'm not sure I can cope	Plan activities to keep you pleasurably occupied in spare time for the first few weeks; plan a couple of visits home

PACKING, TRAVEL AND WEEK ZERO

British universities have many venerable and colourful traditions. One of these is that on one weekend every year, large numbers of cars arrive at the university, usually driven by proud parents and weighted down with the belongings of the nervous student. It's a fine recipe for stress, and for the sort of language which makes the tradition colourful. (There's another set of traditions that affects overseas students, who normally arrive by taxi or bus in the small hours of the morning, in the rain; we discuss those in Chapter 10 about mature students, part-time students and overseas students.)

In an ideal world, if you were going to a university which wasn't too far away, you could sweet-talk your parents into a reconnaissance trip a few weeks in advance, when parking and restaurants wouldn't be clogged with new students, and you could treat it as an enjoyable day out. In reality, you'll probably have to settle for detailed map work in advance, setting out in good time, packing a picnic in an icebag, and being prepared to park somewhere less than wonderful. It's also a good idea to think carefully about which belongings you actually need – you'll probably acquire a lot more during your first year, and end up with piles of clutter. Many students live at home while doing their degree, which at least spares them from this set of hassles, though usually at the cost of other hassles. They may experience other problems, of course. A significant difficulty is often that of negotiating house rules when you are legally an adult, living with your parents. This is an issue for anyone over 18 living in the family home, but is probably made more difficult when you know that other 18-year-olds, living away from home, have a lot more freedom than you do. It's worth talking things through with your parents before you reach 18, and clarifying new ground rules, if you need them. Another possible issue is that because you are living away from the university campus, it may be difficult for you to socialise with other students. You may experience a double whammy in your social life if your best friends from home are away at other universities. A bit of forward planning, such as arranging to stay over sometimes with a friend who lives on campus, may mean that you can get more involved in university life. Take consolation from the fact that you will probably continue your homework habit from school, and so may get significantly more work done than your fellow students who have to contend with the distractions that campus life brings.

What should you pack? It's worth remembering that it's not like going to Antarctica – there will be shops, so if you forget your toothbrush, you'll be able to buy a new one. However, if you arrive in the middle of the night because of transport nightmares, or if you're unable to get to the shops for the first couple of days, then it's advisable to include enough basics to keep you going. The following list includes things that most students find useful. It assumes you'll be in a hall of residence providing you with meals in your first year, which is what most universities offer; you will obviously need other items if you're in self-catering or private accommodation. Check with your university or landlord in advance about what equipment is provided and what you may need to bring with you.

- Coffee/tea/milk/sugar/biscuits; two mugs, two spoons, two plates (useful for socialising in the first week)
- Box of tissues
- Cash (in case the cashpoint machine has run out)
- Toothbrush, toiletries and towels
- Food for two days (including enough cold/dry/tinned food for one day just in case; if you don't need it, store it against future emergencies), plus plates, eating implements, and can opener
- Enough clothes for at least a week
- Paper, pens, folders for filing
- The university's documentation
- Map of the nearest town
- Something enjoyable to fill in your first two evenings – a book, game or activity – in case you end up alone and at a loose end
- A plan of interesting, useful and fun things to do during the first week (you can always modify or abandon this if you end up having a wonderfully interesting, useful and fun time anyway).

Be wary about taking:

- anything of great sentimental value (in case it gets lost or broken)
- anything excessively valuable or delicate (in case it gets lost or broken)
- anything potentially embarrassing, such as your cuddly Mister Squiggles toy (in case it is seen and not properly appreciated by fellow students).

THE FIRST TWO WEEKS

Another venerable tradition is that the first week of the academic year is chaotic. Nobody knows where anything is happening, or when it's happening; timetables change every few minutes; everywhere that you need to be is choked with vast hordes of lost souls heading in three directions at once. There are various unproductive ways you can react to this. You can express anger, and complain to The System at eloquent and sarcastic length about how nobody appears to know how to organise anything; you can sink into despair, and feel inadequate because you don't understand what's happening; you can give up and head down to the Union for a coffee or something stronger. None of these is particularly helpful, and they're likely to raise your stress levels sooner or later, rather than reduce them.

A more sensible approach is to apply a bit of thought. How likely is it that every university in the country happens to be incompetent in the first week? Not very; it's more likely that there's an underlying reason for the chaos (which there is, in the form of the inherent difficulties of timetabling without clashes when you don't yet have complete information about which students are doing which modules, but we'll spare you the grisly details of that problem). That being so, anger and sarcasm aren't likely to fix anything or win you any friends. How likely is it that anyone will manage to get to all the right places at the right times, against this backdrop? Not very; it's wiser to prepare yourself mentally for missing at least one thing, and accepting that this can happen through nobody's fault. If you miss something important, then it's polite and professional to get in touch with the responsible person as soon as possible, apologise for having missed it, and ask what you can do to catch up.

In the next few sections we work through some of the areas which tend to bring stress in the first couple of weeks and look at ways of dealing with them.

Academic issues

A classic cause of stress arises from yet another time-honoured tradition, namely that nobody will tell you about the basic principles of academia. A simple example is that nobody will think to tell you the difference between a lesson which you experienced at school, and a lecture, a seminar and a tutorial, which you'll experience at university. A more subtle example is that usually nobody tells you what constitutes 'good writing' in their discipline. This can cause a lot of grief to mature students who are skilled in writing technical or business English, and who can't understand why their beautifully-crafted writing comes back with cutting remarks on it. This section contains a brief overview of the basic tools of the academic trade; you'll probably know 90 per cent of it already, but the remaining 10 per cent might make your life a lot easier.

In the early portion of your school life you're a conscript, and the teachers have the unenviable job of trying to push knowledge into your head. At university, you're a volunteer, and the traditional academic view is that it's now your job to pull knowledge into your own head – in other words, it's your responsibility to learn, not someone else's responsibility to teach you. It's also your responsibility to learn all the necessary skills for your chosen discipline, not just the fun bits. For instance, if you're planning to be a structural engineer, then a potential employer might reasonably expect that you can calculate whether your design will fall down in a strong wind. It's the lecturers' responsibility to make sure that you're exposed to the relevant knowledge; it's not their job to make it fun.

Every year, some hapless first year makes an embarrassing reference to 'teachers' or 'lessons' in front of lecturing staff. The lecturing staff consist of lecturers, senior lecturers, readers, professors and various other roles; the safest bet if unsure is to refer to them as 'lecturers.' Lecturers vary widely in their formality and philosophy; some are formal and aloof, others are informal and approachable (though this doesn't necessarily mean that they'll be generous markers). Some are happy to be called by their first name; others aren't. If in doubt, calling them 'Dr Smith' (or whatever their name is) is usually a safe option.

Universities, university departments and academics come from a proud tradition of independence dating back to the Dark Ages, so they all do things differently. The usual basic units of teaching and assessment are as follows, but expect variations wherever you go.

The lecture involves someone standing on their hind legs and talking at you for about an hour, usually accompanied by enough PowerPoint to drive anyone to tears. Some lecturers take questions during the lecture, others prefer them at the end. Almost all lecturers hate students coming in late and students talking in lectures. If you're bored, have the courtesy to sit quietly at the back, and read a book or think about what you'll do at the weekend or, of course, what the consequences of not listening to the lecture may be. Most lecturers over-run, which irritates their colleagues in the next lecturing slot as well as their long-suffering students.

The tutorial used to involve small groups of two or three students discussing something with an academic tutor, giving the students detailed, individual support. It now usually involves twenty or thirty students, most of whom sit in sullen silence expecting the tutor to pour knowledge into their heads, and two or three of whom sit at the back texting their mates or having private conversations. If you're sensible and moderately assertive, tutorials are a good way of learning more about the topics that particularly interest you, and which may not be covered in detail in the lectures.

The seminar traditionally, has involved a student, or group of students, giving a mini lecture or presentation on a particular topic to an audience of other students and/or staff. The topic was then discussed. Seminars are much less commonly used in this way than they once were, due in part to the unfortunate tendency of the appointed student or students not to turn up. Nowadays, the term is used to describe a number of forms of tuition, most often involving an invited speaker giving a talk, followed by questions and discussion.

The practical involves practising the practical skills required for your discipline – writing software, or dissecting a language, or doing work in the lab. A lot of students view this as a waste of time, and then wonder why they have trouble getting good marks and a good job. A lot of departments react by making practicals compulsory. As well as teaching students, universities also assess them. Assessment takes the form of examinations and of coursework (which itself takes a variety of forms, such as essays, literature reviews, practical write-ups and research projects).

The exam is like the exams you did at school; see Chapter 4 on exams and assessment later in this book.

The coursework often looks like the coursework that you did at school. This can be a problem, because the expectations at university are different from those at school; you might be set the same question, but the type and level of answer expected may be very different. You also need to beware of plagiarism – which means copying material written by someone else and passing it off as your own work. Schools currently appear to vary in how strictly they police this, but universities take a consistently hard line, and will have no hesitation about failing you in a piece of work if you plagiarise. Universities now give explicit guidance about how to avoid plagiarism and how to reference other people's work, but if in doubt, it's advisable to check that you understand this properly. Proper referencing and avoidance of plagiarism are basic tools of your trade as a university student.

The final year project is used by most departments, but not all. It involves you doing a substantial piece of research-based work of your own, supported by an academic supervisor. The research project culminates in a written dissertation. Many students, and some departments, will refer to the whole process as a dissertation. If you view this as a positive opportunity, you can use it to get a foot in the door with potential employers; there's more about this in Chapter 8.

Practicalia

One major stressor is the unknown; another is feeling out of control. You can tackle a lot of the unknown by simply writing down a list of your dreads, and then finding out the answers. (It's a good idea not to put your name at the top of the list; this reduces the risk of subsequent paranoia about whether someone else on your course might find it …) When written down, the list will probably look a lot less frightening – it often contains items like 'What happens if I fail this exam?' or 'Where are the printers?' Most of these questions you'll be able to answer for yourself with a bit of digging through the university's support materials. For the others, you can try an approachable member of staff.

You can tackle a lot of the control issues by doing some basic planning. For instance, you can plan to alternate between late nights and early nights for the first week, so that you have some balance between socialising and getting enough rest. It's a good idea to set aside some time each day during the first week for catching up with yourself – taking stock, planning, or just having some quiet relaxation. Even a very basic plan makes a lot of difference, and puts you sufficiently in control to start making some better-customised plans.

It's a good idea to locate resources as early as possible – printers, photocopiers, washing machines, and suchlike, but also fun resources such as university clubs, local attractions, and so on. Once term starts, it's horribly easy to end up spending all your time in the same few, familiar places, which might be okay, but which are not necessarily going to fill your mind with wonder and good memories, so keep exploring. It's also useful to learn about the support facilities available at the university sooner rather than later, so that if you hit a crisis, you won't have the added hassles of having to find out where to go. There's a section on this at the end of this chapter.

Social life

At school you're stuck with your classmates whether you love them or hate them; if you're unpopular, then it's pretty hellish. University is different; you don't need to interact with other people on the course any more than you choose to, and there are literally thousands of other students who are potential friends, companions, inspirations, and lovers. If you've had a rough time at school, then university can be a wonderful experience of freedom, and a great source of social life; most students end up with life-long friendships that start in their student days. Freedom, however, often comes with a price, and for new students, that price is frequently anxiety about social life in a new environment. Here are some classic anxieties, and things that you can do about them.

Anxiety	What to do
I don't know anybody	Nor do most of the other first years; strike up some conversations with people you want to get to know better
I don't know how to strike up conversations	Read the section below on basic conversation skills
Everyone ignores me	So what? Everyone else has their own preoccupations at the moment. Would you feel happier if everyone was looking at you?
I'm worried that I won't make any friends	Making good friends takes time. It's a good idea to make acquaintances in the first week, while everyone else is in the same boat and is approachable; you can then take your time and see which of them you'd want to have as friends
People will laugh at me because of where I come from/how I speak/what they called me at school/my sexuality/my cluelessness	Try watching a good American sitcom; they usually have at least one unpleasant character who laughs at *everyone*. Avoid individuals of that sort; work on any bad habits that you do have; seek out people that you get on well with. Universities are usually pretty tolerant of diversity (if only because so many of the academic staff are raving eccentrics)

Making basic conversation

If you find yourself living somewhere you've never lived before, in an institution you're not familiar with, interacting with a crowd of people you don't know, the chances are that unless you are very confident and outgoing, you will at times feel lonely and friendless. This feeling is particularly noticeable when everyone else seems to be going around with 'buddies.' Do not be deceived. Some people do make best friends in their first week at university, but the chances are their friendships will change and develop throughout their university life. So how do you go about making friends? Here are some ideas;

- Remember that other first years, however confident they look, are probably feeling as lost as you are.
- Don't be afraid to start a conversation. Most people will not feel intimidated by someone catching their eye and smiling, or asking how they're getting on, and neither of you need to continue the conversation if you don't want to.
- Ask questions. Most people respond well to other people showing an interest in them. 'Where are you from?' 'What course are you doing?' 'Where are you living?' What's it like?' are fairly non-intrusive questions which could start a conversation. But don't interrogate. Give your potential friend a chance to reply.
- Listen about as much as you talk. Sometimes people open up if you volunteer information, as in; 'I'm from Huddersfield, how about you?' or 'I'm reading German, what are you studying?'
- Don't be desperate. Nothing frightens other people off so much as someone who is too persistent or intrusive. It takes time to build up friendships, so get to know people gradually. You're most likely to make friends with people you see frequently, anyway, so you'll have time to do this.
- Take time to assess the context. This is particularly important in terms of sexual relationships, especially if you are not the same age, or of the same cultural background as most of your fellow students, as the following examples will demonstrate:

One of us knew a middle-aged, recently divorced male postgraduate who was under the impression that sexual morals amongst undergraduates were so loose that he would have no problem making sexual conquests. Most of the female students he met found his behaviour offensive and disturbing. It was only after one student took him aside to have a long, serious conversation that he realised how wrong he was. Another friend, a recent graduate, accustomed to the relatively safe informality of university, once made the mistake of inviting a male work colleague back to her flat for coffee after a social event. She discovered that his idea of 'coffee' was very different from her own, and she had considerable trouble persuading him to leave.

Emotions – homesickness and the like

No matter how socially skilled and popular you are, it's still likely that you'll go through some challenging emotions in your first weeks. You'll be at the bottom of the status ladder – there's nothing lower in the university than a new first year undergraduate – after being at the top of the status ladder in your school. That's inevitable, and it's wise to learn to live with it; you'll have the same experience when you start your first job after graduation, and quite possibly have similar experiences when you're promoted into a new role.

You'll also probably be homesick. This isn't a sign of weakness; it's a sign that you care about the people you're parted from, which is not a bad thing. At a practical level, if you feel that you have a reasonable level of understanding of what you're doing at university, and control over your situation, that will reduce the anxiety that can be associated with homesickness – the desire to flee back to somewhere safe and comforting away from a stressful and incomprehensible new world. That can nonetheless leave the feeling that, no matter how much you like university, you still like somewhere else and want to be there. If home isn't too far away, then you can try scheduling some visits there in the first term – again, if you schedule them in advance, rather than fleeing home on the spur of the moment when it all gets too much, then you'll feel better all round.

Part of being at university is the getting of wisdom, and that can involve pain. So do many of the good things in life, there's usually a price for anything worthwhile. One of the things you'll need to come to terms with is that life involves change, and that you can't avoid change forever. Even if you had stayed back home, it wouldn't be the same 'back home' as it was before. You wouldn't be at school any more; many of your friends would have moved away to university or to jobs; you'd be starting a new job yourself, or starting to experience unemployment. That's probably not the most immediately cheering thought if you're reading this in a lake of tears while wishing you were back on the sofa at home watching TV with your mates, so here's a more positive thought. Stay in touch with the good bits of life at home, including your friends; have some pictures and objects around that give you good memories; think about the positive aspects of life at home, and remember that you can go back there when you want to. Do this in a pleasant setting at university, rather than one with bad associations. This should help you to have a balanced view of the good things in both bits of your life, rather than a view of all university things as being bad, and all home things as being good.

Resource location and forward planning

You'll probably run into some sort of minor hassle eventually; when that happens, it's useful to know about the support facilities available to you. It's a good idea to identify what they are in advance, so you can find them immediately when you need them. The academic system can be supportive, to an extent, which often surprises students. All universities have free student support services, such as counselling and financial advice; all universities also have administrative procedures which will take account of students' personal problems when these are likely to affect their marks in examinations and coursework. The sensible thing is to find out about these forms of support as early as possible, so that you don't need to look for them when you're too upset to think clearly. They'll probably be in the student handbook, or failing that, the department secretaries and your personal tutor will be able to tell you. Appendix 2 lists the main support facilities that most universities offer, and has space for you to fill in their contact details.

If external events look as if they could adversely affect your academic work, tell your tutor as soon as possible and ask what you need to do. You may need documentation to show you have been ill, or involved in an accident, for example. Usually you just need to fill in a form saying that you'd like extenuating circumstances taken into account, and to provide some evidence that the extenuating circumstances really exist. Sometimes you might not want any of the academic staff to know the details of those circumstances; the usual way of handling that is to ask the counsellor or doctor treating you to write a letter saying that you are going through distressing circumstances, without saying anything about what they are. (We've said 'usually' only because we can't absolutely guarantee that this applies everywhere, but it's been the case everywhere that we know about.). There's a further section on extenuating circumstances on pages 53–54.

SUMMARY

Almost everyone finds the transition to university stressful for some or most of the time (a few people just find it exciting). It's tempting to agonise about whether you've chosen the right university and the right course, but as long as you've done basic homework, then there's no point in worrying about your choice; it's more important to work out how to make the most of where you end up. You'll probably feel lost and clueless at the start; so will everyone else. You'll also not have your old network of friends; nor will anyone else, and this is a chance for you to grow out of what you were at school and into someone new, with a fresh start in life.

BIBLIOGRAPHY AND SUGGESTED FURTHER RESOURCES

Lucy Clarke and Jenny Hawkins's *Student Survival Guide* (How To Books, 2001) is popular with students, and covers similar topics to this book, but from a different perspective – they write about how to survive student life and enjoy it, whereas our focus is on how to handle the potentially stressful parts of it.

Another valuable resource which is easy to miss is your university's handbooks. When you start at a university, The System usually gives you a lot of written information. Most students are too busy at this point to read it properly, and it then gets lost at the bottom of the filing stack. Usually there's a university handbook and/or a department handbook and/or a course handbook somewhere among it, and these typically contain a lot of very useful practical information about facilities, support, procedures, and so on.

4

Assessment: coursework, exams and stress

(or, How can I do better with less hassle?)

Preventing stresses where possible; learning how the assessment process works. Exam nerves and coursework stressors. Extenuating circumstances; what to do if life events are affecting your work. Handling the outcomes; what to do with unexpectedly good results, unexpectedly bad results and expected results.

Throughout your university life, you will encounter various forms of coursework and exams. These cause a lot of stress to a lot of students. Sometimes the stress comes from uncertainty about what the results will be; sometimes, it takes the form of exam nerves or writer's block; sometimes, it comes after the results are posted, in the form of bad results when you thought you had done really well. There are a few classic sources of grief which come from the first written work and the first exams, most of which arise from not knowing where the differences are between the expectations at school and the expectations at university. Most students learn the differences pretty quickly when they see the results of their first exams and the first coursework, but that isn't much consolation if you're coming up to those first exams and first coursework and are stressed out of your mind by the uncertainty. There are also classic stresses associated with the final exams; many courses include final year projects, which similarly have their own set of classic stresses. We'll start as usual with prevention.

PREVENTION IS BETTER THAN CURE

A major cause of stress is uncertainty, not knowing what to expect. A second major cause of stress is feeling powerless, believing you can't affect what is going to happen. A third cause is feeling ignorant; you feel as if academic life is like a game with lots of complex rules, which everybody else knows but you don't. This section tackles these issues.

Coursework and exams: the background

By the time you've reached university, you'll already have a lot of experience of coursework and exams. That's in some ways a good thing, and in some ways a bad thing. It's good because you'll be familiar with assessment. It's bad because there are some crucial differences between school expectations and university expectations. Unfortunately, it's unlikely that anyone will tell you the differences unless you ask. The result is two types of potential stress.

The first type of potential stress comes from knowing that there are important differences, but not knowing what they are. The second type comes from thinking that you do know what the differences are, or not believing that there are any, and then getting an unpleasant surprise when the marks come out. One variant on this theme is a recurrent problem for mature students entering academia from the world of work; these students are often very good at business writing or business research, and then hit big problems when they discover that there are big differences between good business writing or good business research and good academic writing and research. Knowing about the differences won't prevent stress, but it will reduce it, and it should prevent that horrible feeling of playing a game where you don't know the rules. It's also useful to know that you're not alone – the majority of first term students are in this situation. The accompanying text box gives an informal and approximate guide to markers' likely reactions to common types of answer. (Warning: it's unlikely that your university will use this precise format, so it's wise to ask your lecturers for the actual marking scheme for their modules.)

At this point, you might be wondering about the issue of differences between markers' expectations in first year and final year assessment, which we mentioned earlier. This is an important issue in most disciplines, but different disciplines have different ways of interpreting it, so your best strategy is to find out the situation in your discipline. One simple method is to get your long-suffering student representatives to ask the lecturers to give your group some guidance on this. As a rough rule of thumb, the further you go through your university life, the more you're expected to take the initiative. You might get away with just reading the set texts in your first year, but by the time you reach your final year you'll be expected to read other material as well as using your own judgement and initiative. This other material will often include journal articles and chapters in specialised books, rather than material written specifically for students.

A rough guide to marking schemes

0–30%:	Straight fail. This answer shows no evidence that the student has ever attended the lectures or read anything about the topic; an intelligent passer-by could have written this answer using general knowledge and a couple of technical terms.
30–40%:	Has probably attended a few lectures or read a bit of a textbook, but that's just a guess. Only limited evidence of having put in any work or of understanding the topic.
40%:	Scrape pass. Has shown just enough evidence of learning to be allowed through.
40–50%:	Has grasped the general idea; fairly harmless, but not someone you'd show off to an important visitor.
50–60%:	Okay; has a fair grasp of the topic and has done a reasonable amount of work.
60–70%:	Good. Has a good grasp of the topic, or has worked hard, but probably not both.
70%–80%:	Excellent. Really understands the topic well, has worked hard and intelligently, with good original insights.
80%–100%:	Outstanding; has worked hard, and read widely and intelligently. I wish I'd thought of some of the points in this answer.

Classic stressors in first year assessment are uncertainty about expectations, and sometimes unpleasant surprises when the assessment results are significantly worse than expected. There's some advice about these topics towards the end of this chapter, and you might find it useful to read the sections in Chapter 2 on handling uncertainty and on unexpected bad experiences. Another common source of stresses on many courses is the final year project or dissertation, which is based around independent work helped by a supervisor. This is a book-sized topic in its own right; one useful strategy is to read one of the many books about doing your undergraduate project, and another is to persuade the member of staff responsible for projects to have a drop-in session where people can ask questions that they're too embarrassed to ask in public. A key thing is to remember that your supervisor is there to give you guidance and act as a mentor; if you keep that in mind, then they should be the best source of advice and reassurance.

Clashing deadlines

In an ideal world, there would be a reasonable interval between the due dates for each piece of coursework in a semester, and your lecturers would never suffer from human frailty. The reality is different. Why is this, and what can you do about it? Deadlines clash because the number of modules being assessed across the university is usually larger than the number of possible due dates, and quite a few of those modules will be affected by factors outside the lecturers' control. The number of interactions, knock-on effects and suchlike for students doing joint honours is so large that it's usually not feasible to co-ordinate dates except for the two or three most common modules on a given course. Where does this leave you as a student? It leaves you knowing that the problem will almost certainly hit you sooner or later, so it's wise to prepare for it. It also leaves you knowing that this is a problem largely outside the control of the individual lecturers, so there's usually not much point in wasting energy complaining about it. You're better off saving your strength for battles that you are more likely to win. Here are some strategies that can help.

Try to prevent clashing dates

There's a fair chance that you can prevent clashing dates for at least the most common combinations of modules. A good way is to do this via the student representatives for your year. As soon as you know the due date for the coursework from the first of the commonly shared modules, you can ask your student representatives to contact the lecturers on those other modules, passing on that date, and asking politely if they could avoid setting their own deadlines on that date. This is particularly useful to lecturers if the modules involved are in different departments, with which they don't normally have much contact. In an ideal world, the lecturers would be doing this by themselves, but it's not an ideal world, and if you take initiative politely along these lines, you might be able to make everyone's lives a bit better.

Plan backwards

A classic cause of stress is discovering that the communal printers are all queued solid at the point where you want to print off your coursework. Most people leave things till the last minute, and this leads to last-minute queues; it also often leads to equipment breaking down because of overload. It's a good strategy to set yourself a personal deadline a few days before the official one, and then plan your time backwards from that. Even if you over-run by a couple of days on your personal deadline, you'll still be finished by the due date. A related issue is to keep backups; a lot of students lose their work just before the deadline because of hard disk crashes and suchlike.

Plan your time

Sometimes it's better to do one piece of coursework first and another second; other times, it's better to switch between them. A good strategy is to sit down with a piece of paper or a spreadsheet, and work out which things you'll need to do for which coursework. For example, if one piece of work depends on something that you'll need to order, such as an inter-library loan, then it makes sense to put that order in as early as possible, and then spend time on the other coursework until the item arrives. It's also a good idea to schedule in some rest time and some spare time, so that when something over-runs, you can absorb that in the scheduled spare time.

Useful strategies for handling the academic issues in assessment

Read the instructions in the coursework/exam questions; they're not just the examiner's opinion

A surprisingly high proportion of students don't read the instructions at the start of the coursework or exam properly, and proceed to answer a question that was never asked in the first place. This usually leads to a bad mark or a fail, since you're marked against what you were asked to do, not what you decided to write about. Something to be careful about is an automatic reaction to a particular phrase, regardless of context. So, for example, computer science students who see the word 'website' often jump straight into designing a website, even if the coursework specifically states that they should not design a website. It's wise to read the instructions, do something else for a while, and then re-read them slowly to check that you really do understand what's required. If you're not sure, then ask the lecturer or exam invigilator politely for clarification.

Plan your answer

Being keen to start and to get the assessment out of the way is understandable, but jumping straight into the answer is not the best strategy. It's wise to remember what you're being marked on. You're normally being marked on what you write, which is true, relevant and, most importantly, not known to everyone on the street. A lot of students suffer needless grief and perplexity because of that last criterion. It's a particularly common problem for mature students and for students coming into academia from industry. In the outer world, it's usually considered desirable to write plain English with as few technical terms, references and 'ifs and buts' as possible. That's understandable. However, you don't get a degree just for having general knowledge. The university assumes that you have general knowledge anyway as your starting point; the purpose of academic assessment is to find out how much specialist knowledge you have gained about a topic, above and beyond what is known by people on the street. The way to show that knowledge is via precisely the things that are normally shunned in writing outside academia – references, technical terms, 'ifs and buts' and so forth, as explained above. When you're planning your answer, therefore, it's important to think about how to demonstrate your academic skills in the answer.

The markers can only give you marks for what you write on the page, so you need to get it there. One useful strategy is to do a first rough outline of your answer based on general knowledge. After you've done that, you then go through the outline, making sure to include things that demonstrate your academic knowledge and which need to be included in the answer – technical terms, references, mention of rare cases that need to be considered, and so on. It's also advisable to think about whether the obvious structure for the answer is in fact the correct one. Sometimes the professional's response is very different from the 'general knowledge' response. The same issue applies to examination answers.

Once you've done the pre-final draft, it's a good idea to use the highlighter test. This involves printing off a hard copy, then going through it with a highlighter, highlighting phrases and sentences which could not have been written by a member of the general public (references, specialist terms, 'ifs and buts' and so forth). These are usually the parts which get you the marks, since they demonstrate what you have learned through being on the module. As a rough rule of thumb, the more highlighter, the better your chance of a decent mark. After the highlighter test, you can help yourself further by checking the regulations about format, presentation and so on, to ensure that your work follows the regulations. If you've word-processed your answer, as is usual with coursework, then you should also apply the spell-checker. If there's time, you might be able to persuade a friend with a good grasp of spelling to check for errors that the spell-checker will miss (such as 'there' for 'their') in exchange for some chocolates or equivalent. If you happen to be good at spelling, and have already done your coursework, then you might be able to build up a decent-sized chocolate stash by offering your services in this way. (Important note: if you're going down this route, remember to check the regulations about collusion, in other words, unfair collaboration. Most institutions allow you to have your spelling and punctuation checked in this way, though they also usually require you to state in writing that you have done this; they do not usually allow your mate with good spelling to give you advice about factual errors.)

Extenuating circumstances: practical solutions

Gordon was once involved in the case of a student who diffidently asked whether the examiners could make any allowance for the fact that he'd recently had an operation on his spine, and had written his exam answers standing up, leaning the paper against a wall, because he had steel plates in his back which prevented him from sitting down. The university system, whatever its imperfections, does at least have mechanisms for taking account of any external events that might reasonably be expected to affect your marks, and in this case the examiners did make appropriate allowance (they would have also given the student a medal if they'd been allowed to). This process goes by different names in different universities, but is usually some variation on 'extenuating circumstances.' If you've had an accident or bereavement, or been ill, or been a victim of crime, or any of the other unpleasant things that life throws at human beings, then the system can make allowance for it, provided that you let the system know officially.

The usual way of doing this is via filling in a form. This may come across as a cold-blooded bureaucratic example of adding insult to injury, but that's not the intention. The intention is to prevent unscrupulous individuals abusing the system by claiming extenuating circumstances to make up for having done no work for the last year. One of the depressing things about being on examination boards is the number of cases where students have made up tear-jerking stories of extenuating circumstances which turn out to be untrue. One of the encouraging things about the exam boards is the amount of helpfulness they usually show to those students who are genuine cases. However, they need some way of knowing who is a genuine case, which is where the procedures come in.

If you have extenuating circumstances, then talk to the appropriate member of staff, and fill in the appropriate form. The precise details vary between universities; if in doubt, ask someone knowledgeable and approachable on the staff. The key thing is that you'll need to supply some evidence to confirm that your story is true. That's something that often worries students, but the system has ways of handling difficult cases. If the extenuating circumstance is something you really don't want to talk about, then there are usually procedures for handling this. For example, most exam boards will accept a letter from a doctor or counsellor which says that you've been through a traumatic event, without saying anything about what that event was. Similarly, if you're a victim of crime, then the police can supply documentation to show that you've reported a crime which is under investigation. The key point is to help the system to help you. If you suffer in silence, you'll suffer once from the event, and then suffer again from being academically assessed without any allowance for the event. Talk to someone, and then they can help you through. None of these things on its own will prevent stress, but each of them improves your chances, and gives you more control. The next section looks at exams, and ways of handling them.

Handling assessment: exam nerves and writer's block

Exam nerves

If you suffer from exam nerves, you're not alone. A lot of other students go through the same problem. It affects students right across the spectrum, including the brightest and most able. Because it's so widespread, it's received a lot of attention, and there are well-established and effective ways of tackling it, which will be well-known to the academic support people at your university. We describe some of these techniques in this section.

A lot of students don't seek help for exam nerves, and then feel guilty, stupid and inadequate because they haven't asked for help when it was available. There's a perfectly understandable reason for being in this situation. It's much the same dynamic as dealing with a phobia about, say, spiders. Asking for help with a spider phobia involves having to mention spiders. If you're phobic about them in the first place, then you're going to be understandably reluctant to start a process that is apparently all about the one thing you most dread. We say 'apparently' because the reality is rather different. The most widely used approach for tackling problems of this sort involves relaxation therapy, and this is based around taking things at a pace you're comfortable with. It's an extremely enjoyable sensation – a bit like lying in a comfortably hot bath, at peace with the world. It's usually fast – two or three hour-long sessions will quite probably be enough to transform your life radically for the better – and usually effective. If you're affected by exam nerves, then we strongly recommend that you talk to the student support people about it, preferably early in the term so that you have plenty of time to sort things out well before the assessment season. An added bonus is that once you've learned how to use this approach, you can apply it by yourself in other stressful situations; you can also use it in normal life to produce a feeling of calm well-being. The text box below contains some specific tips about ways of reducing or preventing stressful exam situations.

Before the exam

- Reconnoitre and get positive associations; scout out the usual examination room well in advance when it's empty, finding out where the crucial locations are (toilets, places where you can leave bags and coats, and so on). If possible, spend a few minutes there thinking positive thoughts (to give you some good associations with it).
- Plan in advance; decide how much time you're going to spend reading the questions and planning the questions.
- Make sure all your pens, pencils, and other stationery items are in good working order, and that you have spares in case something breaks.
- If you have exam nerves, plan your rewards you'll give yourself after the exam – a reward for going into the room, another reward for reading instructions and planning your answers, a big reward if you voluntarily do something that raises your pulse rate, like asking the invigilator for information; another big reward if you write an answer for every question and stay to the end.

(Continued)

During the exam

- If you have exam nerves, do your relaxation exercises for a couple of minutes when you have the opportunity.
- Read the rubric (instructions) carefully, twice. Make sure you know how many questions to answer, and which ones are compulsory.
- If exam nerves are still a problem, do your relaxation exercises for another couple of minutes. If you feel yourself tensing up at any point during the exam, do them again; it will be time well spent, and will help you get a better mark because you'll be working intelligently and purposefully.
- If you find exams a struggle, you can reward yourself during the exam by using positive imaging – imagining yourself on the beach, or out with your friends, or by self-praise – telling yourself how well you've done, or by relaxing your muscles for 30 seconds. Use these mini rewards after you have completed a part of the exam; after planning your timing, planning the answer to a question, or finishing a question. The idea is to associate doing the exam with positive, calming thoughts, rather than negative, stressful ones. Be careful not to be lured into daydreaming, though.
- Decide which questions you're going to do.
- Plan how long you're going to spend on each question. Budget in a few minutes of spare time.
- Plan your answer to each question, making sure you have at least something to say for each part of any multi-part questions.
- Make sure you've included technical terms, facts and references within each answer, to show that you know relevant things that an intelligent person on the street would not know.
- If you're not sure what a question means, ask the invigilator for clarification. The person who wrote the exam paper is on call during the exam, for precisely this sort of situation.
- If you'd prefer not to ask for clarification, then you can start your answer by writing down the possible interpretations, and saying which one you're using.
- After each question, check that you've done all the required parts of it. Don't leave any parts blank – even a sketchy answer to one part can be enough to tip you over the borderline. In a worst case, a few bullet points, a mind map or even your answer plan could be enough to get you over that borderline.

If you've planned rewards for yourself, and earned them by doing the required things, then make sure to give yourself those rewards afterwards; you'll have earned them.

Writer's block

Writer's block is when you try to write something and your brain stubbornly refuses to produce any usable words. It's not much fun at the best of times, and it's less than wonderful if it strikes you in an exam or when you're rapidly approaching a coursework deadline. Fortunately, there's a lot of good guidance available on this problem, for the elegant reason that it's a particular problem for professional writers, who go on to write at great length about it once they've got over it. The suggestions below are a few of the main approaches, the first five of which you can use during an exam. Most of them aim to get you writing something, even if it's rubbish to start with; once you've broken the logjam, the quality of the writing usually improves. Even if it doesn't, you're still better off submitting something lack-lustre than if you submitted blank paper. Don't forget to scrap the paper you've used to remove your writer's block. You would not want it to be handed in with your answers.

- Deliberately write something wrong, so that your subconscious comes raging out, telling you what you should have written instead.
- Write about something completely irrelevant, to get your subconscious started on producing something relevant instead.
- Draw a picture, such as a mind map or a line of boxes, where each box represents a section of what you're going to write. Label each box, and draw labelled arrows to show connecting themes between each section.
- Write five sentences summarising the main points you're going to make. Then write five sentences about each of the first five sentences.
- Imagine you are explaining the idea in a conversation with another student, or your parents, or some other figure who is not going to be judgemental about your answer. Make notes on what you said and use these as a framework for your written answer.
- Set up a line of sweets, and allow yourself to eat one for each line you write.
- If possible, go away and do a useful displacement activity, such as cleaning the grot out of the plughole in the bath. Your subconscious will probably soon feel motivated to sit at a nice clean keyboard and write some words.

Handling the aftermath

Usually, your assessment results will be pretty much what you're expecting. By the end of your degree, you'll have enough experience to predict fairly well what your grades will be in a given topic. With your first assessment, though, there's a lot more uncertainty, since you're now playing under different rules. Most people don't handle uncertainty well. If your results are better than you expected, then that's usually straightforward; if they're worse than you expected, though, that's often a very different story. So, what can you do about it?

The first thing is to have a strategy for dealing with the uncertainty. If it's stressing you a lot, then one effective strategy is to pour your energies into something useful which will take your mind off the waiting. If you can't face anything related to academia in the first couple of days after the assessment, then a useful displacement activity is a good second choice – for instance, catching up on washing and cleaning, or getting your diary up to date so you don't miss any birthdays among family and friends. The next thing is to have a strategy for dealing with the outcomes. It's not a good idea to think that you'll play it by ear after you've received the results. If the results are unexpectedly bad, then you're not going to be in much of a state to make big decisions. It's better to work out your plan A, plan B and plan C in advance, so that you know what you'll do for each of the possible outcomes. Make sure each plan has something positive going for it, rather than being a miserable second best. The following chapters give some more detailed suggestions about ways of handling this.

One question which occurs to most students is why the results take so long to come out; many students find themselves harbouring suspicions that their department is simply incapable of organising anything, or can't be bothered. The reality is that universities take assessment very seriously, with assessment time being a frenzy of activity. The assessment process, however, involves several stages of marking, checking the marking, making allowances for extenuating circumstances, and double-checking everything. After all of this has been done, then the marks are official and can be given to the students. As you might imagine, this takes some time. One way to think of it is that every day it takes for the results to come out is another day in which someone is sweating away to make sure that your work is marked properly.

Dealing with problems

Plan A: better results than expected
This is not usually a problem, but it's worth thinking about what to do if it happens. For instance, you might realise that there are possibilities now open to you that you had previously believed to be out of your reach; if so, do you want to go for those, or do you want to stick with your current goals?

Plan B: the results you expected
This is not usually a problem either, but can be if the results are not good ones, since it can restrict the opportunities open to you. It can also be a problem if well-meaning friends and acquaintances have assured you that you will do well, and are now embarrassed to find they were wrong. This is why you need a plan. Find out ahead of time about options open to you with

your less-than-ideal results, and you will feel more in control. Deal with your embarrassed friends by discussing your practical plans together. A reasonable treat is in order.

Plan C: worse results than you expected

We normally use a two-stage response. After we've checked that we haven't misread or misunderstood anything, and that the reality really is worse than expected, the first stage is to feel extremely sorry for ourselves for the rest of the day, and have a thorough wallow, to get the emotion out of our system. An emotional response is perfectly normal in such circumstances, and trying to stifle it or ignore it is unlikely to be helpful in the long run. If possible, we treat ourselves to an evening of comfort therapy; chocolate, a social drink, a favourite film, some relaxation and centring exercises (described in the appendices). Some people like to write a bit of fiction in which the person they consider responsible for the bad result suffers horribly (though if you do this, be sure to destroy the draft, or at least to make very sure that the offending individual cannot be identified; English law is pretty fierce on libel). There's a fine dividing line between a social drink and getting drunk. Getting drunk is not a good strategy; at best, it leaves you poorer and with a hangover the next morning, when you most need a clear head, and at worst you might do something extremely stupid while under the influence, and land yourself in a much worse situation – for instance, waking up in a police cell, or in hospital. With the reassurance and wallowing out of the way, it's time to move on to the second stage.

The second stage begins the next morning. It involves asking what you're going to do about this situation. You might have worked this out already, while waiting for the results. If you haven't, then this is the time to start. There are two main things to think about. One is how this affects you in purely administrative terms – what options are open to you and what options are closed. Another is what you can learn from this, with a view to growing as a person. One thing to check is what options the system offers you. This may seem blindingly obvious, but surprisingly few students check the regulations about this sort of thing in advance (or at any other point). It may be that a particular bad result is no impediment to where you want to go. If you have a scrape pass in a module where you were expecting a distinction, but you don't need any more than a scrape pass in that particular module to continue with your chosen path, then it may still be an unpleasant surprise to have the low mark, but it won't get in the way of what you want to do. You will usually have at least one opportunity to resit the piece of work. As usual, taking advice from a knowledgeable and approachable member of staff is usually a wise move. They'll have seen a lot of other students going through exactly the same thing, and will be able to help you see the situation in perspective. They will also probably be able to suggest options that had not occurred to you. In theory, your personal tutor should be able to do this, but if you don't get on well with them, then you might want to ask someone else, such as student support services.

Moving on

The world is imperfect, and throws a lot of bad things at most people in the course of a lifetime. Most people make at least one huge mistake in their life. That's normal, and part of being a human being. It's important to measure yourself against a sensible standard. What good mentors and potential employers are interested in is not so much whether you make the occasional mistake, but what you do afterwards. Do you fall apart, or do you pick yourself up, learn from it, and move on as a wiser and more capable person?

At the time, failing an exam can feel like the end of the world. One way of putting it into context is to imagine that you've been flying home to tell your parents the bad news, and the plane has to do an emergency crash landing. You and the other passengers and crew survive and walk away unscathed from the tangled, burning wreckage. In that context, how important is the exam mark going to feel? Exam marks and coursework marks feel very important at the time because you're so close to them. In the greater scheme of things they are not so important, and are far from being the only factor determining whether or not you have a successful career or a happy life.

For example, failure in one subject may simply mean that you picked the wrong course. It is quite possible that you will be allowed to switch to a similar course, or even another degree entirely. You will need to discuss this with your tutor, who will be able to advise you on the course to choose and the steps you need to take.

You may still be able to achieve your original aims by an alternative route. For instance, say you're absolutely dead set on a PhD. You'll normally need an upper second or first class pass in your first degree to be accepted, but even that's not invariable; there are ways of demonstrating your ability after graduating with a lower second or a third, and getting onto a PhD via that route. So, significant findings from a final year research project, a ground-breaking investigation into a famous author's early life, undertaken in your spare time, or a project for an employer demonstrating your ability to tackle independent research, may be sufficient to convince a university to take you on to do a PhD.

Even if you are unable to complete your degree, it is not the end of the world, even if it may feel like it at the time. If you are unable to get the kind of job you originally wanted, think carefully about the alternatives. You may still be able to find a way into your chosen career, but by a different route. Many prospective employers are more impressed by signs of initiative, capability and determination than by the class of degree you got, or whether you got one at all. Be aware that you will need to demonstrate that you do actually have initiative, capability and determination, by achieving something, not by simply telling a prospective employer that you have those qualities. A year on VSO (Voluntary Service Overseas), or carrying out a market research exercise for your local library, or refurbishing a women's refuge – activities relevant to the job you want, and which other people can testify to in a reference for you – will carry weight with most employers.

So, how do you learn the right lesson? One good starting place is to ask the module tutor to give you some suggestions about how to improve things. Listen, don't talk. It's tempting to try to persuade them that your answers in the exam or coursework were actually right, but it's highly unlikely that this is the case. More likely you've misunderstood something, so careful listening is the answer. Sometimes, it's simply the case that a particular topic is one that is not your strong point. We can't all be brilliant at everything; the qualities that make you good at one thing are often precisely the qualities that make you bad at another. It's a good idea to ask yourself whether you're playing to your strengths, and moving your life in the direction that's best suited for you. On that encouraging note, we'll move on to the next chapter.

SUMMARY

Most students find exams and coursework stressful. Few students systematically find out what is expected of them, and how best to handle assessment. A key principle is to get tangible evidence onto the page showing that you've learned things you didn't know before you started the module. If you have exam nerves, then there's good support available at all universities from the student support services. It's usually easy to treat exam nerves and phobias. Some time spent on this is likely to be one of the best investments you ever make.

BIBLIOGRAPHY AND SUGGESTED FURTHER RESOURCES

There are numerous books on study skills and exam techniques. We've listed three typical good examples.

A. Naik's *The Little Book of Exam Calm* (Hodder Children's Books, 2000); like all the Little Books, it's less than ten centimetres on a side, and easy to slip into a pocket or bag if you want to have some calming thoughts near to hand during the day. It contains numerous short, clear tips and thoughts for anyone worried about exams.

Dominic O'Brien's *How to Pass Exams: Accelerate Your Learning, Memorise Key Facts, Revise Effectively* (Duncan Baird Publishers, 2003) is popular, and has a lot about learning and revision techniques.

Dawn Hamilton's *Passing Exams: A Guide for Maximum Success and Minimum Stress* (Thomson Learning, 2003) covers similar ground, but with more emphasis on doing it with less stress.

5

Survival skills, relationships and social life

(or, Will I survive and will anybody love me if I do?)

Moving into private accommodation. Basic survival skills. Clothes and identity. Food. Status, self-image and identity. Maintaining old relationships from pre-university life. Starting new relationships. Uncertainties about the present and the future.

Some stressors are easy to identify: a looming coursework deadline, an unexpected bill, a warning letter from the landlord. Others are not always easy to identify at the time, or arise gradually, which can make them trickier to deal with: for instance, wondering whether you've chosen the right course or the right university, or trying to hold together a long-term relationship with someone that you now only see at weekends. This under-the-radar type of stressor will feature repeatedly throughout this chapter, which covers the subtle stresses involved in dealing with other human beings. But first, we will address the issue of how to keep yourself housed, fed, clothed, clean and safe.

SURVIVAL

Moving into private accommodation

It's more than likely that when you start university you will be offered accommodation in a hall of residence. Universities are very aware that new students have enough things to think about without having to worry about keeping body and soul together. But if you have been offered a place through the clearing system, or are a student at a university with an inner-city campus, or have finished the first year of your course, you may have to arrange your own accommodation. Moving into private accommodation for the first time can be a great, liberating experience or very stressful. It can be both at the same time. The typical worst-case imaginings go something along the following lines. You aren't able to view the place yourself because of some last-minute hitch, and you ask a mate to look at it for you. When you arrive with your gear, you discover that he's found a flat above a brothel guarded by threatening-looking bouncers. The place is a mess, there are cockroaches and fleas, the wiring, gas and plumbing look downright dangerous, your new flatmates are drunken, loud and even more threatening than the heavies downstairs, and the alleged rent didn't include various compulsory extra payments. You can't lock your room, and your belongings vanish. Shortly after you move out, you hear that the police have dug up the basement of the property and have arrested the landlord after discovering bodies of former tenants buried there. We've actually had most of these stories reported to us directly, including the one about the brothel and the one about the bodies in the basement, though the brothel story was at second hand. So, what can you do about this situation?

In terms of preventing problems before they can arise, the answers are pretty obvious. List the things you're worried about, and work out how to avoid them. Most or all of them can be avoided by a bit of forward planning and forethought; for instance, if you have a friend who's staying in decent accommodation, then you can simply ask them to let you know if a vacancy is coming up. Similarly, you can keep an eye open for rooms in good areas. When you inspect a property, take along someone who is sensible and knows what to look out for. If you're worried about what the area is like at night, then drive through it with a friend (so that one of you can look at the neighbourhood while the other drives; if it turns out to be a rough area, you'll be glad that you're driving rather than walking). As for suitability of flatmates or housemates, one sensible strategy is to team up with friends who are likely to be good to live with, and to rent an entire property jointly. If you're worried about affording somewhere decent, because prices are high in the area, then start thinking ahead about saving some cash to bridge the gap. It's also wise to find out in advance the essentials about the law of landlord and tenant – university advice centres usually know a lot about this – so that you don't have the stress of uncertainty if the landlord mentions something odd-sounding about the rental conditions.

There's still scope for hassle and stress even after you've sorted out the things above, since human beings can be difficult to live with at close quarters. Undergraduate students typically don't have much experience of day-to-day life at close proximity with anyone other than their family, and can often be innocently unaware of mannerisms or acts of thoughtlessness which drive everyone else to think of murder. A classic example is cleaning – often it ends up being done by the same person, who does it with an increasing sense of resentment, until they explode in a shower of emotion in front of their clueless housemates. Just having a cleaning rota can prevent this problem, as well as helping to keep the place looking acceptable. Another classic problem is a housemate playing loud music, especially when there's a coursework deadline looming and everyone else wants to concentrate. This is where basic assertiveness skills, described in Chapter 2, are invaluable.

Once you've found somewhere to live, and moved into it, you need to stay alive from one day to the next. That's what the following section is about.

Basic survival skills

You need to keep yourself fed, clothed, clean and safe. For some reason, there's a surprising spread of abilities in these regards; some students are brilliantly organised in their basic survival skills, other students are good in some skills but poor in others, and yet other students are so generally clueless that it's a mystery how they've managed to survive long enough to reach university. Fortunately, there are books available on all these topics; once you've got the hang of the basics, then you can move on to the more sophisticated stuff if you want. First, food. We have not gone into detail about the kind of household items and equipment you will need to stock up on if you are living in private accommodation, as individual circumstances vary considerably. Most universities will offer advice to undergraduates fending for themselves for the first time. It is, however, worth practising half a dozen simple recipes which are quick to make and which use no more than two pans, during the period before you leave home.

Food

There is a wide variety of opinion on what constitutes a good diet. Essentially, you need to eat, or your body goes wrong, and eventually you die. You need to eat a variety of things, or you don't get enough nutrients, and you get sick. The usual view of a balanced diet consists of a staple vegetable that gives you calories for energy (such as rice or potatoes), some other vegetables to give you vitamins and minerals necessary for preventing scurvy and other diet-related disorders, and either a hunk of meat or a helping of high-protein vegetables or dairy products to give the body what it needs for its own repair and maintenance. If you're a vegetarian or vegan you'll probably be eating foods containing vitamins, minerals and trace elements, but will need to be careful to get enough protein. Your body is wired up to like various things that are good for you in small doses and bad for you in large doses (particularly fats and sweet things). If you have a reasonably balanced diet, you're likely to have enough energy and to feel good (if you don't, you won't).

Food planning

Eating vegetables generally works out cheaper than eating meat or convenience foods, and gives you a much wider range of nutrients and less fat. If you baulk at the idea of becoming vegetarian, you can always add a small amount of meat to a vegetarian dish for flavour. Since local butchers who will sell you small amounts of meat are these days a dying breed, divide up your supermarket pack into small amounts in freezer bags and freeze for later use. Browse vegetarian cookbooks and learn culinary techniques from them. If you find vegetarian cuisine too bland, go for a cookbook which is lavish with herbs and spices; eastern vegetarian recipes tend to be much tastier than western versions. You can buy a wide range of grains and beans cheaply from wholefood shops (watch out for health food shops, they can be pricey) or, if you club together with a group of other people, from wholefood distributors. Cheap, fresh vegetables and fruit can be picked up at the end of the day from markets. Look for reduced items in supermarkets.

There are a lot of claims about the effects of diet on well-being, such as claims that you should take vitamin supplements, or that many people have unrecognised food allergies. Most of these claims are controversial; some look as if they may be right, some are downright dangerous. An unsurprising but solid rule of thumb is that most things are okay in moderation; another good rule of thumb is that just because something is good in moderation, that doesn't mean that it's even better in large quantities. It's possible to do yourself significant damage by taking too much vitamin A, for instance. If you think that you may have a food intolerance, or some other diet-related issue affecting your well-being, then it's wise to seek proper professional advice and information, rather than blindly following the latest fad.

Clothing

Clothes are another feature of life about which there is much diversity of opinion. At one extreme are fashion victims; at the other are people who use clothes as camouflage to hide from a world that they find threatening and out of their control. In between these extremes, choice of the right clothes can help your self-esteem and can also make your life a bit easier. A friend with a good awareness of the finer points of dress can be invaluable for this. A good short-term stopgap is to have two, or preferably three, unremarkable but acceptable outfits (one to wear, one in the wash, and one for emergencies such as the washing machine breaking down), and a set of smart, understated clothes for job interviews and formal events; you can build up from that step-by-step. Clothing plays an important role in identity for many students – and it's tempting to spend a considerable part of your meagre finances on it. However, if you've taken on board the ideas about budgeting in Chapter 7 you'll realise that your expenditure on your wardrobe will be limited. There are a number of ways round this problem. If you're not too scrupulous about working conditions in the third world, cheap, trendy clothes are currently easily obtainable in a range of shops and from market stalls. If you have scruples about who made what you wear, you can pick up some superb bargains in charity shops; they often have factory seconds – clothes which have some minor flaw but are otherwise excellent and extremely cheap.

The way to tackle charity shops, if you've never done so before, is to find out where they all are, and visit them regularly. Good days are Tuesdays and Wednesdays, since people often donate their old clothes to charity shops at weekends, and the charity shop staff frequently put them out for display on a Monday. If you can befriend staff and tell them what you're looking for, so much the better, since they will often be happy to set stuff aside for you if you're a regular. Since people who regularly give clothes to charity shops tend to give to the same shop – often because it's on their way to work – you'll probably find a couple of places that sell the sort of thing you're look-ing for and can make them the focus of your regular visits, which saves time.

Another source of good, cheap clothing is the post-Christmas and summer sales. Go early on the first day if you're after something specific at a bargain price; go during the last couple of days if you're not fussy – you can some-times pick up things for pennies. If you're short of cash, it can be tempting to buy clothes you're not enamoured with just because they're cheap. Don't. It's not a bargain if you don't want it or won't wear it. A better strategy is to buy one expensive item that you love and wear it all the time. A friend of Sue's once bought an eye-wateringly expensive pair of jeans which looked fantastic. Whilst they were being washed and dried, the friend wore her one skirt. The jeans lasted her for an entire year and worked out no more expen-sive than buying two pairs of less-than-wonderful jeans that would have lasted twice as long, but were much less loved.

Cleanliness, tidiness and optional godliness

An old proverb says that 'cleanliness is next to godliness.' Certainly, keeping clean is a Good Thing and most students are well aware of its importance, so we won't say much about it. What we will say is that the temptation to rele-gate washing the dishes, or washing your clothes, to the bottom of your 'to do' list is strong when other more interesting occupations are on offer, so a few tricks are worth bearing in mind to avoid situations such as having noth-ing in the house fit to eat from, or no clean clothes to wear. The first is to fix a time when you do the washing-up (say, once a day) or do your washing (once a week, perhaps). That way, you're unlikely to feel compelled to wash every dirty coffee cup left on the kitchen worksurface, nor are you likely to run out of cups. If you are in self-catering accommodation, and sharing kitchen equipment with other students, it would be worth setting up some ground rules such as having a washing-up rota, or each person washing up after they have been cooking. If you have such a huge backlog of washing-up, washing or ironing that it is beginning to feel intimidating, the simple expedient of dividing it into smaller, more manageable amounts and doing one lot each day until the mountain has disappeared, can be very effective in restoring your feeling of control.

We will, however, say something about the related topic of keeping tidy – if you have your stuff organised efficiently, then there's less risk of it being broken or lost, and you have more feeling of control over your life. It's also useful practice for later life. In a lot of jobs, being neat is an important professional skill, and there are serious accident risks if you leave things lying around. Similarly, most people much prefer to work with someone who has things organised. If you find you are getting obsessive about tidiness or are finding it stultifying, you could try keeping most of your stuff organised and leaving one area, such as your desk or a cupboard in disarray 'to remind yourself that you are a human being' as one of our student colleagues put it.

Safety

Keeping safe is also a Good Thing. Universities do not want their students to endanger themselves, and they regularly issue warnings about avoiding risky situations such as walking home alone late at night, meeting strangers alone in an unfamiliar place, watching out for drinks being spiked, not taking illegal drugs and so on. What the university may not tell you is how damaging less risky behaviours can be, which is why we mention some of them here. One of the less obvious pitfalls is hanging around with unsafe people who are likely to get you into unpleasant, stressful situations that aren't doing you any good. The classic case is drinking mates who get each other into dangerous or humiliating situations because they think it's a laugh. Humour is a great thing that helps make the universe more bearable and good friends are beyond price, but if you end up in Accident and Emergency in the small hours of Sunday morning, taking up the time of surgeons who are also needed for road traffic accident victims, then you're not having much fun and your acquaintances can't be described as real mates. More subtly, there are people who bully you or who gratuitously say things that damage your self-esteem or who manipulate you into situations where you end up facing problems. These can include anything from feeling pressured into recreational drug use, having unsafe sex, losing money in online gambling, or being involved in vandalising phone boxes to sitting up all night playing computer games or surfing the net, or spending too much time with your boyfriend or girlfriend and not enough time working. If someone is damaging you, then don't include them in your life. Note that we specify people who gratuitously say damaging things, as opposed to people who are trying to help you be aware of areas where you may have room for improvement, such as ourselves. As a rough rule of thumb, if people are suggesting something feasible where there's a good payoff for you at the end, then they're helping you; if they're not suggesting something feasible, and there's no good payoff for you, just an unkind comment about you, then they're not helping.

SOCIAL SKILLS

Status, self-image and identity

Just before you started university, you were probably at the top of, or at least a fair way up, the status ladder in your previous institution – for instance, a lofty prefect looking down on the lesser mortals at your school, or a manager in a company. When you start university, all that changes – you suddenly have to start all over again, at the very bottom of the status ladder. There is nothing lower in the university pecking order than a first year undergraduate, especially one in their first week. The staff may know the cleaners by their first names, and probably have long-standing friendships with them; they won't have a clue what your name is, and will view you as part of a mass of new faces some of whom might turn into useful students some day. There's no point in trying to fight against this – from their point of view, it's a completely sensible stance. If you tell a lecturer that you got 95 per cent for something in your final school exams, they won't be impressed, for the simple reason that you're playing a different game now – it's like telling the basketball coach that you used to be a great under-eighteen rugby player. Phrases such as 'So what?' come to mind. It's much the same if you tell them that you used to be a Senior Assistant Manager in Logistics. That's the bad news. The less bad news is that, whatever its weird and wonderful faults, academia has a strong strand of meritocracy running through it. It's a bit like the science fiction story about the chess player who teaches a rat to play chess. This doesn't generate much interest in the chess club at first, since the rat's opening moves leave some weaknesses on the queen's side. The fact that the rat is a rat doesn't particularly bother them. It's similar with academics and students. Although some academics are less than perfect, there's a strong tradition of ignoring where the student happens to come from, and of assessing them just in terms of merit; a good student from humble origins will be much more highly valued than a bad student from a rich family. Some of this is due to simple idealism; some of it is due to simple self-interest (bright, capable students make your life a lot better if you're a lecturer, particularly if you can get them to do PhDs with you, which will reflect glory on you).

So, what can you do about this? One thing to remember is that first years look much the same as everyone else apart from when they're wandering round being clueless in the first week of their first term. Once that week is over, you're unlikely to be on the receiving end of any jokes about first years – everyone will have other things to think about, like how to get through the workload for the term. Another thing to remember is that it's up to you to earn respect in this particular sector of society – find out the things that show you're worthy of it, and knuckle down to earning it. You'll probably have a similar experience when you go on to whatever you do after university, so it's worth learning to accept that you were born knowing nothing and that it takes time to acquire things that are worth having.

Relationships

Established relationships

Established relationships, and the strain that moving away from home can put on them, can be a significant source of stress for university students, especially if it's the first time you've been separated from your loved ones. First, the unwelcome truth; it's likely that you will not be able to maintain all your old friendships with people from school and home, so you may have to be very selective about who you keep in touch with. If you don't, you may spend a lot of time e-mailing and calling people you have less and less in common with, and miss out on making new friends. The only way to keep friendships going is to communicate, but just as you will be busy with new courses and making new friends, so will your old mates, and with the best will in the world, you'll probably find that you start growing apart from some of them. If you get no response from an old friend, be prepared to put that relationship on hold till the next time you go back home. Sometimes the friendship keeps going as if nothing has changed – some childhood friendships last a lifetime – but you may find that you have less and less in common with some former friends, and that meetings become increasingly uncomfortable for both of you.

If you have a long-term romantic relationship with someone, and you've just started university fresh from school, then you're going to have a challenging time ahead. You'll be trying to put time and energy both into your old relationship and into your new situation; you'll be worried that you may miss opportunities in the first few weeks of term that will not come round again – those first weeks are the ones where it's easiest to make new acquaintances and friends. It is possible to maintain the existing relationship, but to do so, you'll need to be pretty rigorous with your scheduling. Try to discuss with your boy/girlfriend the ways in which you could handle the separation. You'll need to tackle this sensitively, so as not to appear to be the party introducing the possibility of problems ahead, or worse, the possibility of splitting up. Try to agree on times when you can meet (maybe every weekend or every other weekend) and try to alternate venues, so that you can keep up with each other's lives – meeting each other's new friends, for example. Agree times to phone each other. This will free you both up to get on with your lives without feeling guilty. Be spontaneous occasionally, but only occasionally. The odd unexpected phone call is a delightful surprise, but a constant stream of unexpected calls could make your partner feel guilty for not being as demonstrative as you are, or as if they are under surveillance.

Your separation could unfold into several scenarios: you could realise that you can't live without each other and end up with a lasting, committed relationship; or (the outcome you've been dreading) your girl/boyfriend could meet someone else; or (the outcome you've been dreading nearly as much) you could meet someone else; or you could split up after a blazing row; or you could drift apart because you're now leading separate lives. All of these outcomes are possible in a relationship where you are seeing each other every day, of course, and there is plenty of advice available to address them. The problem for you is that if one of the dreaded outcomes takes place, or you are finding separation from your partner intolerable, you may be miles from your old friends and family and not yet have built up a network of trusted friends at university. If the worst happens, and you feel incapable of coping, don't be afraid of seeking the support of a university counsellor. There's a popular misconception that the pain of broken relationships in adolescence or early adulthood is less extreme than in later life. That's simply not the case. Young adults are often in and out of relationships, it's true, but are also less experienced than older adults and have fewer resources to draw on to see them through the crisis. You are more than likely to recover from the trauma, and may realise in years to come that a long-term relationship with your childhood sweetheart would have been a disaster, but at the time, the separation can be devastating. If you feel embarrassed about not being able to cope with it, tell the counsellor that you feel you should be able to cope with the situation but can't, and that you would appreciate someone to talk to.

Old friendships and loving relationships are familiar and valued. The problem is that the world around you undergoes continual change, and so do you, and those friends. Friendships can arise for a wide range of reasons. Sometimes it's because you've met someone on the same wavelength as yourself; if you have similar personalities, those friendships can last for life. Sometimes the friendships arise because you've both been through the same unusual event, which gives you a common bond that again can last for years. Sometimes they arise because you're going through the same situation as someone else, and find them easy or fun to get on with – for instance, surviving school, or having a shared interest in sports, or living near enough to drop in on each other to socialise. Once you're out of that situation, if there's nothing else special to keep you joined as friends, it's quite likely that you'll drift apart. Similarly with loving relationships; you'll change as a person through your teens and twenties, and so will the person you love, so you might find within a few years that whatever once made you love each other has now gone. You'll also be surrounded by new people, some of whom will be a closer match to the person that you've become; your beloved will also be going through similar contacts with new people. You can also change later in life; going to university in middle age can produce the same associated issues. If you're drifting apart from someone special, you may find it useful to turn the situation round, and imagine that you are forced to stay for the rest of your life with someone that you fell in love with at school. Viewed from that perspective, the prospect has some obvious potential drawbacks. Would you find the other person's mannerisms so captivating when they're middle-aged and not a cute teenager any more? This won't infallibly give you a perfect answer, but it may help you decide whether the drifting apart is a blessing in disguise, or whether the relationship is worth fighting for.

Homesickness

On that pensive note, we'll move on to the classic emotions that people usually go through when starting at university (or any new place). You'll probably go through most or all of five stages. First, the honeymoon, when you love everything about the place and are enthusiastic about the people and the system. After this many people go through a crisis, feeling homesick, lost, isolated, lonely and withdrawn. This does not usually last, and you should find that you move on to the reintegration stage when you can expect to become more confident and assertive and start to find fault with the place and the people. The fourth phase is autonomy, which makes you feel more relaxed and able to cope and is followed by the final stage of independence when you enjoy and relish the lifestyle you have. Not everyone feels homesick, and the different stages last for longer or shorter times in different people. If you feel stuck in the crisis stage, seek support as soon as you can. Preparation is the best way to avoid the worst feelings, but if you're already experiencing them, the next two sections should help.

New relationships

The bad news about moving to any new situation is that you could lose some old friends; the good news is that you'll also have the chance to make new ones, who may have much more in common with the new you. Friends come in all shapes and sizes and you will fulfil each other's needs in different ways. Some friends will give you information, some will support you when you are feeling low, others may act as sandpaper to tell you when you are being an idiot and to help rub off those sharp edges. The friends you have in a sports team will probably fulfil a completely different role from your flatmates or a sexual partner. Don't expect one person to fill every friendship need – the person you sleep with may not be the best person to ask for help in revision. An exclusive relationship can be too limiting – what's unkindly but accurately known as a 'gruesome twosome.'

That leads onto the issue of love. Wry observers might class this as an irregular noun: 'my feelings for my beloved are deep, true love; your feelings for that red-haired woman are a passing infatuation; that guy is just feeling crude lust.' When you're in a new place, surrounded by thousands of eligible new people, there's a pretty good chance that you'll encounter this emotion before long. There's usually an initial stage where you can't eat or sleep without thinking about that special person and you worship the ground they tread on. After the initial stage, it will either settle down to a long-lasting feeling of steady love or fizzle out for one of various possible reasons. An old but good cliché is that love is like a fire; when the fire is in the early stages, there are a lot of spectacular flames, which gradually change to a steady heat that lasts for much longer, even though it's not as spectacular. Why do we mention something that everybody knows about? Because the stage of infatuation can involve falling for someone who, at a rational level, is clearly going to be Trouble with a capital 'T.' We could give lengthy advice about this, but the chances of anyone who is infatuated paying any attention to it are pretty slim, so we'll just make the point, and then move on to the less glamorous but more practically useful topic of making new friends of the ordinary sort, which closes this section.

Chapter 3 contained some advice about the basics of starting conversations and getting to know people without sending out too many inadvisable signals. It's a good idea to complement the 'getting to know you' skills with some thought about what you're looking for in potential friends and acquaintances, as mentioned above. It's tempting to choose friends using the simple strategy of identifying the most attractive and the most cool/fun/high-status people who are likely to pay any attention to you. That's understandable, but it's worth also thinking about issues such as finding friends who could be relied on to give emotional support when you most need it, and friends who can help you to explore and develop your inner self as a person. There are also people who are interesting, but quiet, and therefore often overlooked – they can bring new insights into your life, and possibly change it profoundly by helping you see things from perspectives you'd never considered before. That concludes the section on relationships; we now move on to uncertainties.

UNCERTAINTIES ABOUT THE PRESENT AND THE FUTURE

Of course your future is uncertain – everybody's is. Even with the best-laid plans, there always remains the possibility of being struck by lightning next Tuesday. However, that is not very likely to happen, so there's no sense in worrying about it. A more useful way of looking at uncertainties and problems is to view them as opportunities. They then become exciting rather than scary and chances to expand rather than stay at home in a nervous heap with the duvet over your head. The other side of the same coin is having goals. People who are actively embracing life and have clear goals suffer less from stress and are happier than people who just drift.

How can you reconcile having goals with handling uncertainty? That's what this section deals with.

You may be very unsure about your long-term goals at the moment. Here are some ways of sneaking up on the future that could help you crystallize your ideas.

- Imagine that you win a million pounds next week. What would you do, and how would you spend your time as well as the money?
- Think about some day in the distant future. The day is perfect in the sense that it includes all the things you want for yourself, to have and to do. Describe it in detail.
- If you had only one year to live (in perfect health) how would you spend your time?

If you relax and let your mind drift, this sort of fantasy exercise helps with the big picture, to focus more sharply and form goals and aims. Then ask yourself, 'What do I need to DO to achieve my aims?' and your answer tells you what you need to do today and tomorrow and next week. For instance, if you want to be a brilliant barrister, you have to get a good degree to get you into law. That means you need to write a sparkling essay for next week rather than go to the pub tonight. Go to the pub after the essay is handed in. Be sure to keep your final aim in sight. It can seem a very long way from your next exam but each step moves you closer to the goal. That's the basic concept; it's simple, and obvious with hindsight, like most really good ideas. There's more about it in later chapters.

SUMMARY

You may be living independently for the first time, which may mean learning a number of new skills such as finding accommodation, cooking and buying clothes on a very restricted budget. At university you'll be starting afresh, and this will put serious strains on some of your relationships. Although this may hurt in the short term, it's part of a natural progression, and is a necessary part of moving on through your life. As you go through university, you'll change, and you'll grow apart from many of your old friends. You'll also acquire new friends with whom you have more in common. University friendships often last for decades, so it's worth learning to meet new people.

BIBLIOGRAPHY AND SUGGESTED FURTHER RESOURCES

Survival skills

There's plenty of material available about survival skills. One useful strategy is to borrow 'introductory specialist' books from your library for each of the main topics involved in this chapter – for instance, an introduction to secretarial work will contain a lot of good practical information about efficient ways of getting your filing system to work smoothly. Books on specific topics such as basic DIY, cookery and time management are numerous and easy to find. Books on broader topics such as sorting out your domestic organisation as a whole are less numerous. There are some tongue-in-cheek guides with titles like 'household management for men' which can be surprisingly good, but many of these are marketed as Christmas gift books, and go out of print almost immediately. It's worth looking around for books on the bigger picture of sorting out your lifestyle and infrastructure, since changes in one part of your infrastructure will have implications for other parts, and it's useful to have a clear picture of how those bits fit together.

A useful book on basic housekeeping, by Tom McNulty, is *Clean Like a Man: Housekeeping for Men (and the Women Who Love Them)* (Three Rivers Press, 2004), which is supported by a web site at www.cleanlikeaman.com The book's basic premise is how to spend the minimum of time on housework while still getting it done, but the original tips and techniques are useful, especially if your parents are turning up at short notice.

Inge van der Ploeg's *Clear the Clutter: Make Space for Your Life* (Floris Books, 2004) helps you deal with the physical infrastructure of your household (removing clutter and organising your belongings) and the ways in which the infrastructure interacts with your lifestyle (making it physically easier to do the activities that you really want to do). It's easy to read, thoughtful and interesting.

For some reason, there seems to be a dearth of books on household management – Isabella Beeton compiled her famous nineteenth century work for this very reason. There have been various books on this topic over the years, but they don't seem to stay in print for long. If you can find a copy, *The Home Expert* by Dr D.G. Hessayon (1987 edition) gives clear, comprehensive information about the home and its contents, including topics as varied as how to fix common problems with windows, and how to lay a table with seven-piece cutlery settings. There are also sections on home security, on the basics of buying and selling a house, and on budgeting and utility services.

A more recent book with similar content is *Household Management for Men* by N. Browning and J. Moseley (Cassell, 2003).

For food and nutrition, there are numerous books and online resources. One example is Michael van Straten's book on healthy eating, *Super Foods* (Mitchell Beazley, 1999), which looks at foods with therapeutic properties, as well as providing guidelines for balanced eating.

Two books that are widely recommended for novice cooks are:

Jocasta Innes' *The Pauper's Cookbook* (Frances Lincoln Publishers, 2003), which has been a favourite among students for decades. It's packed full of good recipes for people who don't have much money.

Delia Smith's *Delia's How to Cook: Book One* (BBC Books, 2000) starts from scratch, for people who literally don't know how to boil an egg, and works up clearly and systematically from there.

Relationships and social life

It may be the topic of numerous jokes, and getting on for a century old (it was first published in 1937), but *How to Win Friends and Influence People* (Mass Market Paperback, 1990) is still excellent in its way. The author, Dale Carnegie, is explicit about not using the book as a cynical way of manipulating people; he focuses on the need to understand things from the other person's point of view, which remains good advice today.

You could also try Steven Chandler's *50 Ways to Create Great Relationships: How to Stop Taking and Start Giving* (Career Press, 2001) for a practical guide.

6

Major life events

(or, What do I do if something really bad happens?)

General features of major life events – bad timing, surrealism, being caught off balance. Specific life events: bereavement and loss, endings of relationships, accidents, injuries and illnesses, and crime. Moving on after life events. Sources of help and support.

This chapter is – in one respect – different from the others. It's about things that by their very nature are difficult or impossible to prevent. For some of them, such as death of an elderly and much-loved relative, you can know in advance that the event will happen, but not when that will be; others, such as being involved in a serious accident, might never happen to you at all. You can, however, prepare for such events, and that's what we'll focus on in this chapter. It's important to note that this doesn't involve callous, cold-blooded calculation – quite the opposite. One of the most striking features of major life events ('life events' for short) is that they tend to happen at the most surreal times – for instance, you get the phone-call telling you that a favourite aunt has died when you're in the middle of a noisy party, or you discover that one of your friends has just taken an overdose at the precise moment when a van driver knocks on the door with a parcel for someone who moved out last year. A lot of life events happen during exams – given the amount of time that universities spend on exams, this is understandable, but it's difficult to handle emotions such as loss and grief at the same time as trying to sit an exam that you've been dreading for months.

For these reasons, it's wise to have some contingency plans in place so that you can handle the life event properly, with a chance to work through the accompanying emotions. It's also wise to be prepared for things that can happen to other people, so that you can at least offer some help if something bad happens to a friend and you're the one they turn to first. This chapter describes key features of life events, and works through the main life events, such as bereavement, the end of a relationship, crime and accidents. It doesn't set out to be a crime-busting guide or a first aid manual, but it should give you enough basic information to remove some of the uncertainty that characterises these situations, and to give you some feeling of control and direction.

HOW TO RECOGNISE A MAJOR LIFE EVENT

Life events usually show some or all of the following features while they are happening:

- they occur at the worst time you can imagine
- they involve at least one aspect which is utterly surreal
- they catch you off balance
- at least one friend reacts bizarrely to your news.

Bad timing

A classic reaction to a life event is to think 'Why did it have to happen now?' You get the news of a bereavement in the middle of a celebration; you have to face a situation that demands a cool, clear head when you've just had a night out and a couple of drinks; you have to handle a difficult and demanding problem when you're in the middle of exams. It's a bit like the way that the place where you're going always turns out to be on the edge of the map. In a sitcom, this sort of timing can appear funny; in real life, many people can and do start to wonder seriously whether they're cursed and unlucky, or whether fate has it in for them. The answer is that by their very nature, life events will tend to happen at bad times. The reason is much the same as the reason for the edge-of-the-map effect. How much of a map would you class as being 'the edge'? Probably somewhere between an eighth and a quarter of the way in from the edge. If you do the sums for that fraction multiplied by the four edges of a page, then you suddenly realise that about half of the points on the map are going to be near one edge or another. It's the same with life events. If you turn the question round, and ask what would be a good time to encounter a life event, it's unlikely that you'll come up with many times that are free of other things going on. In the cold light of day, this seems pretty obvious, but if you've just had two bits of bad news in quick succession and you're lying awake and upset at 3am then it might not be so obvious, which is why we've spelled it out here.

What can you do about it? You can be mentally prepared for it, by knowing that things do happen at bad moments, but that doesn't mean that you're accursed. You can also build some buffer zones into your life, to reduce the number of peripheral issues that might get in the way otherwise. For instance, if you have to rush home to visit a sick parent and you don't have any money for the journey, then that's an added problem; if you have to rush home to visit a sick parent, and you have some emergency money left safe in your bank account, then that's one problem less. Other buffer zones include a couple of days' worth of emergency food in the kitchen cupboard and an evening or two each week with nothing scheduled; there are other examples in the various sections on planning and life skills. These strategies are not just useful for major crises – they can make life easier when you have several simultaneous assignment deadlines to meet.

Surrealism

If you're unlucky, you might be the first person to arrive at the scene of an accident; it's no fun. As if that isn't enough, there's a fair chance that it will happen on the night when you're on your way to a fancy dress party, done up as Hel, Norse goddess of death. It happens for much the same reasons as the bad timing of life events; there are so many surreal things happening at any given point in life, that there's a fair chance that one of them will coincide with a major life event. That's bad enough if you're the one being surreal; it's worse when the surrealism is coming from someone else, and you have to work out whether they're serious or not. For instance, a colleague in psychiatric nursing in the midlands told us about a client who claimed to be a prince in a West African state; she afterwards discovered that it was completely true.

What can you do about dealing with an emergency in a surreal situation? If you're the one in the fancy dress at the roadside, then you can give the emergency services a quick, simple statement that you were on your way to a fancy dress party, and then go immediately into your 'calm capable professional' mode while you tell them the situation. They're used to surrealism, and once they've pigeonholed you as a capable member of the public, things should be fine. If, on the other hand, you're the one faced by a guy in a gorilla suit telling you he's just seen someone suspicious lurking down the side of your house, then you have the difficult job of playing it by ear. There are no easy answers for this one, apart from a general principle of 'if in doubt, and there's a risk of crime or blood, call the emergency services', and another general principle of 'if in doubt, stay somewhere safe and don't go anywhere alone with a stranger.'

Being caught off balance

Life events tend to catch you unawares, and then to unfold faster than you can keep up with them. This can add to the immediate stress by making you feel that you've lost control; it can also add to the long-term emotional effects by reducing your opportunities to work through your feelings. This is a situation where centring exercises can be particularly helpful. You can go to the bathroom on the pretext of answering a call of nature, take some deep breaths, and work out a rough set of priorities and strategies that will put you back in some sort of control. From there, you can create more time and more control for yourself – for instance, by delegating tasks if you've ended up in charge, or by telling the person in charge that you'd like half an hour to clear some practical tasks out of the way, such as making arrangements for someone to feed your hamster or collecting your washing from the laundrette. Once the immediate crisis is over, it will probably still be some time before everything is back to normal. It's wise to budget time and emotional space for this – clear as much as you can from your diary, and schedule in time for practical matters like making statements to the police, visiting victims in hospital, and activities that will help calm your emotions.

Inappropriate reactions

It's emotionally wrenching to hear that, say, your much-loved and elderly dog back at home has just died; it's salt in the wound if a supposed friend falls about laughing at the news, or appears to shrug it off and starts listening to music. Unlikely? On the contrary, it happens surprisingly often. Why does it happen? One common reason is that the other person doesn't know how to handle the situation. One way that people often handle awkward situations is via humour: fine if you've just spilled coffee over your lap at the start of a meeting, but not appropriate if you've just heard that someone has suffered a bereavement. Another way of handling these is by changing the subject: again, fine if someone is discussing something like their choice of underwear, which you don't want to talk about, but not so good if someone wants to talk about their feelings after being mugged. Most of the people around you will be fellow undergraduates, typically in their late teens or early twenties. A lot of them won't have much experience of life's nastier side, and a lot of them, particularly the young males, will not yet have fully developed frontal lobes, which handle the relevant empathic social skills; the frontal lobes can take quite a while to finish developing. Some fellow undergraduates will appear cool and capable precisely because they stay out of awkward emotional situations which they don't know how to handle, making them the worst people to turn to for help while they paradoxically look like the best sources of capable understanding.

What can you do about this? One thing is to assess your friends carefully, and learn their strengths and weaknesses, so that you know who you can turn to for emotional support when you really need it. Something to watch for is that after someone has helped you through a rough patch, and seen your raw emotional underbelly, you might feel very awkward about seeing them again in a social setting, and feel tempted to avoid them. Avoiding them can come across as very ungrateful, so one thing you can do is to give them a tangible sign of appreciation, such as a carefully chosen gift, and to tell them that you'd prefer not to talk about the episode for a while, if that's okay with them. If they're mature enough to have been of help, they should be mature enough to understand how you're feeling. On that positive note, we'll move on to some specific life events that life can bring.

SPECIFIC LIFE EVENTS

We've tackled four main classes of major life events, and we've tackled them in the order below for a reason. Bereavement and loss have a surprising amount in common with the ending of a relationship; accidents, injuries, illnesses and crimes also have a surprising amount in common with each other. We'll return to those shared features in the section on moving on. Because of the similarities, there's a certain amount of repetition in some of the sections below, since we're assuming that if you've just suffered a death in the family you won't be much inclined to read the section about endings of relationship as well as the one on bereavement.

Something to be aware of is that some events can be more stressful than you might expect. The researchers Holmes and Rahe asked people to rate their experiences of stress from life events on a hundred point scale. Unsurprisingly, bereavement was at the top; something that many people find surprising is that moving house is a close second. Another surprise is that unexpected good news can be as stressful as unexpected bad news; both bring changes to your life, and it's usually the change itself which is the stressful part, rather than the direction of the change. Stressors can also be cumulative; several small things can add up to as much stress as one really big stressor, so it's wise not to underestimate them. A little time spent sorting out small stressors will give you a larger buffer zone if a big stressor happens to come along.

Bereavement and loss

If you lose someone, or something (a pet, a job, a relationship) that is important to you, you may be surprised by the complicated mix of feelings that you experience. There are five stages commonly experienced after a loss (though not invariably all five in this order; we've described the most common sequence, since this will affect most people). First there's a numb, shocked phase when you don't believe what has happened and may deny it: 'This is not happening to me.' Then there's the second stage, of anger and guilt. Many people are surprised by the feelings of anger and guilt that come in this stage. They may be angry with themselves, God, or the person that has died or left. A stage of bargaining comes next: 'If I do this, you'll do that.'

This can produce superstitious rituals. After Helen's mother died, she feared losing her boyfriend as well. Her superstitious behaviour showed up in her having to have the bag he had given her with her at all times, including when she went to the toilet, even in her own home, for about two years.

The most familiar stage of sadness, grief and depression of mood comes next, followed by the final stage of acceptance of the loss. Often, all the stages are experienced, sometimes only a couple. They do not necessarily come in the order described and some can be quite short-lived. As a rough guideline, the loss of a close relationship will take most people about a year to come to terms with. Events such as anniversaries are likely to make feelings re-surface for years afterwards – birthdays, the date of the loss, a visit to a place with strong associations. It is possible to get stuck in one of the stages, so sometimes a person will be very bitter after divorce because they are hanging on to their anger. Or people are stuck at the grieving stage of their loss for years, well beyond the usual period for healthy grief at the loss of a loved one. Counselling helps if this happens. It's increasingly common for people to hold services celebrating the lives of the dead, and this concept shows how it's possible without contradiction both to regret the loss of someone loved and also to feel the joy of having known them.

Endings of relationships

When an important relationship ends, you can expect to go through some or all of the stages of loss described for bereavement – disbelief, anger, bargaining, sadness, acceptance. It's much the same whether it involves loss of a person, loss of a pet, physical separation or emotional estrangement. What you tell yourself has an important effect on the way you feel. If you brainwash yourself with thoughts like 'He has left me, he doesn't love me any more, so I am unlovable' then you are quite likely to feel very low and take a long time to get over the loss. You can improve the situation by programming yourself with a more helpful message, such as 'Although he was very important to me, he is only one person and I am still the same lovable, lovely individual that I was before he left. I now have an opportunity to meet someone better.' Write some or all of these thoughts down in a private place and study them. Then when you feel low, remind yourself of them. All your other friends still like you, don't they? Just one person changed their mind. There's an exchange in the film *Twister* which sums this up neatly. The about-to-be-divorced heroine is talking bitterly about her ex-husband to her wise aunt. The aunt says, 'Yeah, he didn't keep his part of the bargain after he left you.' The heroine says, 'What was that?' and the aunt replies 'To pine away and die, miserable and alone.' That's a good description of the underlying emotions most people feel. It's made brilliant by the heroine's retort 'Well, was that so much to ask?' Loss happens, and it hurts; good things, though, also happen. It's important to keep a balance and not let grief wash everything else out of your life.

Accidents, injuries and illness

Many accidents and injuries are avoidable and most are quite rare. Tell yourself that they are unlikely to happen to you, because they are low probability events. Take sensible steps to avoid them and then forget about them. Basic health and safety procedures will prevent most accidents – things like keeping the floor clear of trip hazards, not trying to lift heavy objects down from above head height, and being careful with boiling water and electricity. Serious illnesses are also low probability for most students and, if you look after your body, you further reduce the probability of being laid low. (As you reach for your fiftieth cigarette and your tenth drink, you could ask yourself, 'Where am I going to live when my body caves in?')

Case Study from Susie: Barbara had an overwhelming fear of lightning. During storms, she would cover all the mirrors in the house then climb into the under-stairs cupboard till it was all over. She never went out in the afternoons in summer for fear of being caught in a storm. But she lived close to the city centre – no-one had ever been struck nearby. Maybe she needed to know that on average only nine people die of lightning strikes a year in the UK, mostly on golf courses, sheltering under trees – in other words, you're pretty safe from lightning, especially if you don't play golf. If knowing a statistic changes your view of a fear, then you can get on with your life; if not, then you should consider treating it as a phobia and doing some desensitisation, as described in Chapter 2.

Car accidents are much more frequent than being struck by lightning so you need a slightly different tactic for them if you're worried about the risk of being involved in one. Take all sensible precautions to make your trip as safe as possible; wear a seat belt, check tyre pressures, take rest breaks and never let anyone who has been drinking drive you. Consider taking an advanced driving test. All these things reduce the odds of you being injured. If you have an accident, even if it is your fault, it is helpful to keep a sense of proportion. A natural reaction is to tell yourself 'I'm a lousy driver', but you need to counteract that by driving again as soon as you have the opportunity and noting how many times you drive safely. It may help to note down each accident-free journey and give yourself a treat after say, twenty safe driving trips. After you regain your confidence, stop counting – you will have regained the 'good driver' bit of your self-image.

That's the brief overview of preventing accidents and illness and of keeping them in perspective. What happens if you're one of those unfortunate people to whom something bad does happen? Serious accidents and illnesses can have a profound negative psychological effect, since most people deep down have a secret belief that they're invulnerable and that bad things won't actually happen to them. Being confronted by your own mortality and vulnerability can undermine this cosy belief, and push you into a new, scary world. Interestingly, many people who have come through accident or illness say that the experience gave them a more realistic view of the world. If you find yourself recovering from injury or serious health problems, then it's useful to know that any feelings of unease are perfectly normal, and it's wise to view them as part of learning and growing. It's also perfectly normal, and wise, to consider going to a professional to work through those feelings.

Crime

Like accidents, crime involves loss of control, usually suddenly and traumatically. This can be profoundly unsettling, because it makes you question your previous assumptions of personal invulnerability, and raises questions about which parts of your life you actually can safely take for granted. Crime is also likely to make you feel personally threatened, sometimes with intrusive fears such as worrying that the person who mugged you might find out where you live and break into your house. It can also leave you feeling humiliated, dirtied and devalued. If you've been on the receiving end of a crime, then you need to contact the appropriate professionals. The police have got their act together about dealing with people who've suffered sexual attacks, and there are good support services available. This is a situation where discreet, competent friends are worth their weight in gold – it makes a lot of difference to have someone quietly capable with you when you're reporting the crime and going through the subsequent processes.

Dealing with the feelings produced by crime is beyond the scope of this book; it's something for other specialists to handle. However, there are related issues that involve stress, so we'll say a bit about those here. One is that people tend to significantly overestimate the risk of crime. The classic fear – of a criminal stranger in a dark place – only rarely becomes a reality. What is more common, and what tends to produce inflated fears, is the stranger whom you happen to find frightening, in a dark place. Your feelings of fear may be real and strong, but that isn't the same as saying that the particular situation was a near-miss as far as crime statistics were concerned. The violent-looking male on the lonely street might have been on his way home to the wife and kids, and scowling because he'd just had a hard time on the late shift at work.

Unfortunately, telling someone about statistics doesn't usually change their feelings immediately. So, what can you do about it? The answers are fairly obvious; take sensible precautions to make your accommodation visibly secure, make sensible arrangements about travel and transport, and don't get into unwise situations, such as hitching lifts alone if you're female. There's a lot of easily found solid, useful information about crime prevention which is put out by the police and other bodies; following their advice will make you feel that you've done something to get your life more under your control.

Case study, from Susie: When Mike arrived it was clear that he was very angry. When he sat down he told me that on his way to our meeting, in his new car, a kid had thrown a stone at him. It had bounced off the bonnet, skidded across the windscreen and careered off the roof leaving a small ding in his bonnet. He was seething. Mike's unhelpful habit was to make the worst of any situation and give any silver cloud a dark grey lining. After he had let off steam for a few minutes I said, 'Wow, Mike, you are the luckiest man alive! It could have killed you, **but** you are OK. And the car might have been badly damaged if you had swerved off the road, **but** it had just a small dent. How fortunate. So, tell me about your new car.' He was happy to talk about performance, economy and so forth, and to congratulate himself on his lucky escape.

This process is called 'Reframing' and helps people see the positive side of events. Mike's habit of dwelling on the negative aspects of things made him gloomy and miserable company. Focusing on the positives has a lifting effect and improves mood. The word 'but' in a sentence cancels out everything before it; in this case, the message to Mike was 'You're okay. It was just a small dent.'

MOVING ON

Life events are often followed by strong and frequently unsettling emotions, which are often more unsettling because of being unexpected. Life events can make you all too aware of things that you previously hadn't thought about, or whose full implications hadn't hit you. That can lead to reassessing large areas of your beliefs about yourself and about the world, which can be a difficult and painful process. Moving on after a traumatic life event is likely to involve support from a professional. It can take a while. It may be months rather than weeks before you feel that you can pass for normal on the outside. Inside, there are two main routes you can take. One is to worry round in circles like a hamster in a wheel, trying to force what happened into an old framework that it won't fit into. That's the stuff that novels are written about – tragic feelings going unresolved for decades. The other route is to understand that some part of your view of the world didn't fit what happened, and to rebuild your view of the world so that it can handle what happened. It's a bit like a crash barrier at the roadside on a steep hill. If you're the engineer responsible for the barrier, and you find that a vehicle crashed right through it and down the hillside, then you can either spend the rest of your life agonising about it, or you can build a better crash barrier, which will save the next vehicle. Bad things happen; you can't prevent all of them, but you can do your best to prevent as many as you reasonably can, and then move on with your life. Many people respond to traumatic life events by the equivalent of setting up a charity to fund better crash barriers – that doesn't take away the crash which motivated them, but it does give the feeling that the crash didn't occur in vain, and that it led to something better in the world.

SUMMARY

Major life events can be very challenging, and have a habit of coming at the worst imaginable times, often in bizarre circumstances. It's wise to find out where the main support services are in advance, so that you're ready if you or a friend should ever need them. It's also wise to know your friends, so that you know which ones you can turn to for which types of problem – a friend who is great for one type of problem may not be much use for another. Life events can be profoundly unsettling, so be prepared for some far-reaching disquiet when a life event strikes. Life events can be grim at the time, but they're part of life and growth.

BIBLIOGRAPHY AND SUGGESTED FURTHER RESOURCES

Sources of help and support

The specific support services available will depend on where you are and what happens to be in the vicinity. Universities typically have good information about what's available, and have good 'first port of call' facilities such as Nightline, where you can at least have someone to talk to. It's a good idea to find out the contact details for the main services, and put them together in an easily accessible place, so that you can find them immediately if ever you do need them. If you do this in your first week in new accommodation, then it's done, and you can get on with life. In Appendix 2 we have included a section where you can write down useful contact details. Another tip is to collect the relevant leaflets, fliers and cards and keep them in an envelope by the phone. You can also find phone numbers for a variety of support services on noticeboards in the students' union or at the Health Centre. Some useful sources of help and support are listed below.

- Victim Support, for support after a crime
- Rape Crisis Centre
- AIDS helpline
- CRUSE (deals with bereavement care)
- Gay helplines
- RELATE is widely perceived as offering marriage guidance counselling, but it also deals with unmarried couples experiencing relationship problems with divorce counselling and psychosexual therapy
- Church-related support – all universities have clerics on campus from at least one faith, and many students (including atheists) who are nervous about talking to a counsellor find it helpful to talk to a compassionate, sympathetic cleric
- Many localities have free counselling centres which are locally funded, but these are often not widely publicised. Check Yellow Pages under 'Counselling and Support', 'Therapy' and 'Psychologists' or ask your GP or Health Centre or student support service.

Paul Harris's *What to Do When Someone Dies: From Funeral Planning to Probate and Finance* ('Which?' Essential Guides, 2006) is excellent if you're the person who is having to handle the practical aftermath of a death.

Elisabeth Kubler-Ross and David Kessler's *On Grief and Grieving: Finding the Meaning of Grief Through the Five Stages of Loss* (Simon & Schuster, 2005) deals with the emotional consequences of bereavement, via the classic five-stage framework.

7

Finance

(or, Why do I never have enough money at the end of the week?)

Preparation for university: planning and saving. Routine budgeting. Handling problems. Looking forward.

Tactless and unkind people are likely to tell you at some point in your university life that money is like air and sex; it's only a problem if you don't have enough of it. Since these days students are expected to start their working lives in debt, by definition you are unlikely to have enough money and so finance will be a problem for you. So, what's the nature of the problem, and what can you do about it? We've divided this chapter into four main sections. The first is preparation – the big picture of how to set up your finances so you reduce the risk of getting into problems in the first place. The second is routine budgeting and finance – ordinary daily, weekly and monthly money-handling. The third is handling problems if they arise. The fourth is looking forward to the rest of your life, and the role that finance will play in that.

PREPARATION FOR UNIVERSITY

Among the many traditions that occur in societies around the world, one favourite is persuading young people to go massively into debt. One example is bride price; any young man wishing to marry his beloved had to pay her father an obscenely large number of pigs and trade goods (in the case of New Guinea) or cattle (in the case of the Zulu). The main options available to those lovelorn young men were (a) to spend the next twenty years accumulating enough wealth, and then marry her if she hadn't married someone else in the interim, or (b) to borrow the bride price, and then spend the next twenty years or more paying off the debt. Not the most brilliant of arrangements for the young couple, involving a lot of issues about treatment of women, but a great way for The System in their societies to make sure that young people had a solid incentive to work hard and conform. It's tempting to make witty remarks about how such arrangements have been replaced in industrial societies by mortgages and student loans, but we'll resist. The point is that there's a widespread, long-established tradition of young people taking on very substantial long-term financial commitments, so if you're going into debt to pay for your studies, this isn't some weird aberration, or a sign that you're financially incompetent.

It's worth looking long and hard at the options available to you financially, which is what this section is about. There are alternatives other than a standard issue student loan and/or grant (or whatever is usual at the time when you're reading this book since governments have a habit of tweaking the education funding system periodically). You could, for example, be eligible for a university bursary or scholarship or for industrial sponsorship. If you are desperate for cash, be aware that some banks offer interest-free overdraft facilities to undergraduates, and you can, of course, buy things using credit cards. We would advise caution in the case of the last two options because interest rates on credit cards are often high, and, you will, of course, be expected to pay back any money you borrow from the bank.

In addition to these you have other strategies open to you. One is to build up your resources before starting your degree. The resources may be money, but may also take other forms. Why? Because the regulations about loans will change through time; it might be that The System will take account of any savings that you've built up, and reduce your loan accordingly, for instance. In that situation, having money in the bank wouldn't make things much better for you financially. However, in that situation, there would be quite a few advantages in having built up a substantial collection of clothing and items you might need as a student, before getting a loan, so that you didn't have to worry about finding money in your second year for a decent winter coat, music system or computer. Having said that, it reduces your stress levels considerably if you know that there's enough money in the bank to cover common financial emergencies, such as buying a replacement when your laptop suddenly burns out, or travelling home to the other end of the country if there's a family crisis.

Some students save up enough money in advance to fund themselves through the degree; this is especially common with Master's degree courses, which typically last for just one year. An advantage of doing things this way round is that it reduces stress about what happens if you don't find a job immediately at the end of the course. It feels a lot less bad to be unemployed and debt-free than to be unemployed with a debt of thousands of pounds.

Another strategy, which you will need to consider in advance, is to work while doing your degree. There's a number of ways you could do this. You could take a standard three-year full-time degree course and work part-time whilst doing so. In theory this is a good idea, and it's a well-established custom in places like the USA, where most degree courses are designed to allow students to work their way through college. In the UK, however, this approach often ends in tears and stress. The typical pattern is that students start with a small-scale evening or weekend job, then discover that it isn't bringing in enough money, so they start working more hours. This means that they get behind with their coursework. Usually they don't tell the academic staff about the situation till things are really bad, and more difficult to fix. If you end up in this situation, and you clearly care about trying to do well on the degree, the staff and support services will be supportive on the whole. A variant which won't get much support and sympathy is that some students are pretty open about having a part-time (or even full-time) job and thinking that it won't be a problem; this is implicitly saying that the degree is so lightweight that people can get through it in their spare time. Anyone who says this has either missed the point about what's expected in a degree, or has decided that they don't care about doing it shoddily; neither of these positions is likely to win many friends among the lecturing staff.

Another possible strategy would be to take a part-time degree course. A number of universities offer these, and although the degree takes longer to complete, it is possible to hold down a part-time job at the same time. Another option is to take a modular distance-learning course, such as those offered by the Open University or by correspondence courses. These can often be completed a module at a time, which is useful to students who are in full-time employment. Unfortunately, The System in the UK hasn't yet sorted itself out in relation to people working while doing degree courses. Although it looks like a simple concept, there are more complications and knock-on effects than bear thinking about. Here's one simple example; if you're doing a modular course, first taking a module, then working for six months, then doing another module, and so on, what happens if the regulations about pre-requisites for final year modules change while you're part-way through your degree? The implication is that the university needs to keep track of which set of regulations you are running under, which can result in three students doing the same degree, each working under a different set of regulations, depending on the year when they started and how much time they've taken out. Confusing? That's just the simplified version. The upshot of this is that some UK part-time degrees are well thought-through, and some UK employers are sensitive to the issues involved. Other degree course arrangements still have the occasional rough edge; if you're contemplating this route, you might find it useful to read the last chapter of this book, which has more detail about part-time degrees and related issues. That thought concludes the section on preparation; the next section deals with budgeting, and how budgeting fits into your overall life planning.

ROUTINE BUDGETING

The core concept of budgeting is simple. You work out how much money you've got; you work out how much you need; you subtract the second from the first, and see what's left over. That's the core concept; it's not particularly difficult to grasp. So why does it go wrong for so many people? A major factor is that because of the way the human brain is wired up, people tend to overlook things, and tend to be optimistic about the costs of the things that they do remember. We'll now go through some of the more detailed aspects of routine budgeting.

Types of expenditure

Expenditure falls into two types, namely predictable (such as your rent, food bills, travel costs) and unpredictable (for example, having to replace the kitchen ceiling after a pipe burst). Predictable expenditure can be a one-off (such as art materials at the beginning of a course) or repeated (for instance, a travel card at the beginning of each term). Repeated expenditure varies in frequency (such as annual car tax versus weekly grocery shopping). That's the basic picture. So, in theory, you can sit down before you start your degree, and list all the expected expenditures for each year, term, month and week; a quick bit of arithmetic should then tell you what your expected expenses will be for that year. In practice, (a) people forget at least one item and (b) people underestimate regular costs such as the weekly shopping. Some seriously organised people keep track of all their expenses for a year, which then tells them what items they need to include in the budget for next year, even if it doesn't tell them what the precise costs will be (because of inflation, for example). It's a large amount.

On top of this, there are the unpredictable one-off costs and contingency (emergency) costs. For instance, your car blows a gasket and you have to pay to have it fixed, or a favourite aunt dies and you have to spend money travelling to Cornwall for the funeral. It's tempting to blame the universe for this sort of cost, and to bewail your bad luck. A more productive alternative is to consider that when you buy a car, you also buy its mechanical problems, and the responsibility for getting them fixed. A knowledgeable friend could probably give you a pretty good estimate of how much you'll need to spend on car repairs each year – in other words, they're a fairly predictable yearly expenditure, which should go into your budget, rather than an act of God which is so unlikely it is safe for you to ignore. It's an unfortunate truth that you'll probably have to deal with at least one expensive emergency during the time on your degree course, so it's wise to budget for one. That's the standard bit of moralising which descriptions of budgets are supposed to contain – true, worthy, but not always very helpful if you're trying to get by on very limited resources and you already know that you don't have enough money to cover your expected costs. So why have we included it? Partly because a surprising number of students don't actually know how to do a basic budget; partly because there's often scope for better budgeting; partly because there are ways of budgeting which will leave you feeling less stressed and more in control. The example of Ben, below, shows how this works. Ben is determined to manage his money carefully. His tuition fees are covered by his student loan for fees so his budget is concerned with his accomodation costs and living expenses.

Ben's budget*

Income
Student grant + loan for maintenance   £6000

Monthly expenditure
Rent   £200
Bills
    (water, gas, electricity, phone, TV)   £50
Food   £100
Travel to and from campus   £20
Incidental expenses   £100
Total   £470
Annual total of monthly budget   £5640

Annual expenses
Deposit on room   £200
Books, materials etc.   £200
Library fees, IT costs etc.   £200
Clothing   £200
Travel to and from university
    twice a term   £150
Total   £950

Total income   £6000
Minus annual expenditure   -£950
Minus monthly expenditure (x12)   -£5640
Shortfall   £590

*These figures are for illustration purposes only and are not intended to give an accurate indication of income or expenditure for all students.

Although Ben is not planning to stay in his university town during July and August, he will have to set aside some cash for the rent on his room, and over-estimating his budget for monthly expenses will allow some extra money for emergencies. Even if Ben sticks strictly to his budget, he realises he is going to need to earn, or borrow, another £590 a year to make ends meet. He plans to do this by taking on bar work and working during vacations.

What do you actually need? Financial lateral thinking

In the strictest sense, you actually don't need very much to stay alive – warmth, food, water. Anything more is a want, rather than a need. That may sound pedantic, but it isn't. There's nothing wrong with wanting more than that bare minimum, but if you assess your wants against that bottom line, then you have a better perspective, and you realise that much of your budget is about how much you want something, which raises interesting questions about whether your priorities could be improved.

A second major factor is that there are often better ways of getting to the same goal, if you do some lateral thinking. Two of our colleagues lived in London, and asked their accountant's opinion about the best type of car for them. The accountant found that it would be cheaper for them to travel by taxi and Tube – so much cheaper that they could hire a luxury sports car for a fortnight each year, and still be ahead of the cost of running a car in central London. They would also be spared the hassle of finding somewhere to park. We're not claiming that the same will be true for everyone, but it's worth looking hard and systematically at the major items on your budget, to see whether you can find a substantially cheaper way of getting the same job done. It's usually also possible to trim some money off the regular budget; this can total up to a substantial amount over a year. For instance, if you add some inexpensive recipes to your repertoire, then you can probably save a substantial amount on food bills compared to living on 'meat and two veg' or takeaways.

Ways of viewing your budget

It's easy to view your budget as a humourless killjoy. Though understandable, this is a misperception, and one which will cause you stress and hassle in the long run. A better way is to view money budgets and time budgets as your decisions about how you personally are going to make use of your personal resources. 'Making use' includes using those resources to have fun; you should actively include enjoyable activities as a category in your budgeting. That way, when you have fun you won't be rewarding yourself for breaking your own resolutions about your budgets, and getting into a vicious cycle of learned helplessness; instead, you'll be able to enjoy yourself with a clear conscience, and with a feeling that you're no longer a jellyfish being wafted about on the seas of fate.

Ben, the student in our example, was doubtless not overjoyed when he worked out that his student grant and loan combined would not actually cover his living expenses. But being in possession of that information gave

Ben a realistic picture of what kind of lifestyle he could expect at university, and enabled him to plan in advance how to approach his future. He could go straight to university from school being aware that his lifestyle would be quite frugal and he would have significant debts at the end of it. He could decide to spend his gap year working somewhere interesting and save as much of his salary as he could to supplement his student grant and loan. He could start his career, and then take a degree course sponsored by his employer; or take a part-time degree course whilst working; or if he couldn't face the financial constraints, he could skip university altogether. Instead of viewing financial constraints as an act of malevolent fate which he had to make the best of, Ben could view his budget as providing essential information for making decisions about what kind of life he wanted to lead. Having to make unpalatable decisions in advance is preferable to finding yourself unexpectedly unable to complete your degree course because your credit card repayments are so high that you can't pay for accomodation in your second year.

Another thing to remember is that even the biggest decisions in your life are your personal decisions, not fixed points in the universe. It's tempting to think that your university course is a fixed point, but it's actually a choice. If you end up in a worst case situation where you simply can't afford to live while doing the course, then this isn't an impossible and unfixable problem; there's always the option of withdrawing from the degree and returning some other time. That may not be a very wonderful option, but it does exist, and you are allowed to choose it. Knowing that there is a way out of a financial hole can make a lot of difference to your stress levels, and has the added advantage of increasing your chances of finding a better solution, since you'll be able to think straighter.

HANDLING PROBLEMS

Retail therapy versus retail addiction

One widespread method of cheering up a bleak stretch of life is retail therapy; shopping for things that make you feel good, as opposed to shopping for groceries and suchlike. Like many other things in life, it's a good servant (if you have enough money to pay for the goodies) and a bad master (if you don't have enough money). It can also turn into an addiction, and spiral out of control, though this is a comparatively rare outcome. How can anyone get into that situation? The usual pattern is a vicious spiral, where the financial problems trigger greater comfort spending, and the comfort spending triggers worse financial problems, and so on. Shopping isn't the only thing that can turn into an expensive addiction, of course, and there are some suggestions in Chapter 2 on how to avoid and deal with addictive behaviour.

If you're already having problems with excessive spending on feel-good items that you can't afford, then one simple solution is to find different feel-good items that you can afford. This may be something like a doughnut, a game of squash, or watching a favourite film. Remember to give yourself the feel-good item after you've done something virtuous, so that you don't subconsciously reward yourself for feeling miserable (which is otherwise a risk with consolation goodies). A closely related problem is the perception of yourself as being in the dark pit of debt; that's the topic of the next section.

The dark pit of debt

If you're in debt, you're likely to feel as if you're in a deep, dark pit that you'll never climb out of. That perception leads to a temptation to stop trying, and revert to whatever behaviour got you into the problem in the first place. A better way of visualising it is being in a tunnel of debt. The great thing about a tunnel, as opposed to a pit, is that if you stop actively trying to get out of it for a moment, you don't risk falling back to the bottom and having to start all over again. This isn't the same as saying that it's okay to default on any legally binding repayments now and again – it's not – but it is saying that if you keep working away at it steadily, you'll get there. It's a good idea to reward yourself when you reach points along the way, such as half the debt cleared off; it's also a good idea to make sure the reward is something that you enjoy but which doesn't cost much, such as listening to music or watching a comedy show. This will improve your morale as well as acting as a reward. Some people find it useful to pin up a 'debt thermometer' (like the ones you sometimes see outside churches depicting the level of the church roof fund) showing how much they've paid off. This can help your morale, but can be dispiriting in the early stages, when you see how much remains to be paid; if that's the case with you, then you could try breaking it down into small manageable goals, such as the first ten per cent of the debt, and doing a new debt thermometer picture for each new small manageable goal. Again, if you feel your debt is spiralling out of control, contact your university counselling service. Also the local Citizen's Advice Bureau will have trained debt counsellors who can advise you.

LOOKING FORWARD

A common strategy for approaching long-term financial planning is to approach it a step at a time, and only take each step when you can't put it off any longer. If you're a first year undergraduate who has just left school this strategy is understandable. You're quite likely still struggling with the concept that most of the cash you were looking forward to spending on updating your music collection or exploring the nightlife offered by your university town, is rapidly being taken up by expenditure on rent and coursebooks. Unfortunately, finance is one of those areas of life which doesn't live comfortably with spontaneity. Planning ahead – a long way ahead – can make your life much more comfortable, or at least much less uncomfortable, than it would have been if you did no financial planning at all. Financial planning is best tackled in a similar way to life planning – backwards – so we'll start with paying off your student loan.

Paying off your student loan

At the time of writing, many students finish their courses in debt to the tune of £10,000 or more. Ben, the student in our budget example, will leave university with student loan debts of at least £18,000. If his first job commands a salary of £20,000 and in the unlikely event of his never getting a pay rise, he would be repaying the loan at the rate of £38 a month for 25 years, and, because of interest rates, still have an outstanding loan of £19,000 (more than his original debt!) at the end, which would then be written off. Our intention in including information like this is not to stress you further, but to make sure you tackle life as a student with realistic financial expectations. Realistic financial expectations means acknowledging that you are unlikely to be able to afford to lead anything approaching a lavish lifestyle as a student, and that during your first few years of employment after graduation a significant amount of your expenditure could be spent in paying off your student loan – the sooner you pay it off, the less interest you have to pay over the lifetime of the loan. This may affect your choice of employment after you graduate.

Whilst on the subject of long-term financial planning we want to mention briefly some very long-term financial issues: mortgages, families and pensions.

Mortgages

If the word 'mortgage' fills you with dread and foreboding, you are not alone. Like pensions, mortgages can sound complicated to the uninitiated, but, like pensions, the underlying idea is simple. You want to buy somewhere to live but you don't happen to have enough money to do it outright. So you borrow the money from someone who is willing to lend it to you (usually a bank or building society), and agree to pay back their loan, with interest, at regular intervals, usually once a month. Since the amount borrowed is large, there's a lot of interest to pay, and the repayments go on for a long time, often twenty years or more, which is the tedious bit. Mortgages may seem like something which belongs to the distant future for you, but it might be worth thinking about arrangements like this one: Pete was about to start a PhD. Pete's dad took out a mortgage on a house near the university and Pete moved into it with a couple of mates. They all paid rent to Pete's dad. The money from the rent covered the mortgage repayments. When Pete got his first job, he bought the house from his dad, at the price his dad had paid for it three years earlier, and his two housemates continued to pay rent, this time to Pete. This meant that Pete and his mates paid reasonable rents for several years, and Pete got a foot on the property ladder. The details of an arrangement like this need to be worked out with professional advice, because of issues like capital gains tax, but it may be worth thinking about in terms of long-term financial benefit.

Families

The idea of having financial dependents may sound very alien and/or alarming. The key thing to bear in mind is that children are expensive. When you do the sums about how much a child costs its parents between birth and attaining adulthood, it's a lot of money. Don't be misled by (true) stories about newborns sleeping in drawers and parents being able to kit them out from charity shop purchases. Young children can be very cheap to keep. It's when they get older that the expenses start to mount, often because you have to buy a bigger house to accommodate them and support them through university. It's more than likely that having a mortgage and supporting a family won't affect you whilst you are a student, but their financial implications are worth bearing in mind when you are looking for a job. If the idea of living in a suburban semi with a spouse and 2.4 children is your idea of bliss, then you need to think about what kind of employment and what kind of career progress is going to support that kind of lifestyle. If, however, all you can think about is teaching white-water rafting in the Canadian Rockies, or working with your local wholefood co-operative, you will need to bear in mind that you may need to make adjustments to your lifestyle expectations in later life. Which brings us onto our last topic in this section, pensions.

Pensions

If the thought of spending your declining years alone in a decaying bedsit living on toast and tea seems like such a remote prospect you can't even contemplate it, think again. It may not be that different from what you are experiencing as a student. So what can you do to avoid this sorry scenario? Paying into a pension scheme (either your employer's or a private scheme) is generally viewed as a better option than keeping cash under your mattress. The underlying idea of pension schemes is a simple one. A group of people pay into a pension fund over a long period; the fund is invested and grows; when a member of the group retires, they are paid a pension by the fund. The more they have paid into the fund, the more they get out of it. The longer you've been paying into the fund, the smaller each of your contributions will need to be to get a decent pension in the end. If you don't start paying into it until you're five years from retirement, a huge slice of your salary will need to go into the fund to get a living pension out of it – and that's usually just at the point where you will have one child at university, one getting married and another producing your first grandchild, all making claims on your finances. So it is well worth starting to pay into a pension scheme as soon as you can when you start work – then your contributions won't need to be a huge sum. Pension planning is a specialised area of expertise so you will need to talk to a financial adviser about it before deciding what to do, but once you start thinking about employment after university, it's worth getting pensions on to your mental agenda.

SUMMARY

Finances are a major problem for many students. Basic financial planning is a good first step; looking at financial decisions as part of your broader life decisions is an even better step. Thinking ahead about long-term financial planning can significantly reduce your stress levels even if it's only because you are aware in advance of how much things cost. There are sometimes useful solutions that come from lateral thinking about finances from first principles. Finances should be a servant, not a master, and planning helps you to take control of this.

BIBLIOGRAPHY AND SUGGESTED FURTHER RESOURCES

Keith Houghton's *Manage Your Student Finances Now!: Balancing the Budget at University and College* (Vermilion, 2003) is an example of a book about the core principles of financial management for students.

It's also worth looking out for books and websites which give specific advice about grants, sources of funding, and so on. These are updated at regular intervals as the relevant information changes with time. For obvious reasons, books of this sort soon become out of date, but they can be invaluable while they are still relevant. We won't give further examples, since they'll soon go out of date, but we would strongly advise making some time to look for them. Your university student union will probably be able to advise you about this.

8

Life planning

(or, What do I want my life to be, and how do I get there?)

Principles of life planning. Time management. Priority management. Planning for the long term and short term. Preparing for life after university.

Some of the material in this chapter will be familiar, since the same issues crop up in a variety of contexts. This chapter brings together a number of topics into what's intended to be a coherent framework for sorting out your life and making the most of it on your terms. The first section deals with the big picture and general principles of life planning and life skills as a whole. The second section deals with finer-grained day-to-day organisation. The third section deals with planning ahead for your life after university.

PRINCIPLES OF LIFE PLANNING

Like budgets, plans are good servants; some people worry about the risk of their becoming masters. An easy way to avoid this risk consists of two simple steps: (a) keep your plans simple and (b) update them fairly often. They don't need to be detailed or complex to be useful; for instance, you can have a plan for the next fifty years which simply consists of 'Work for thirty years, then retire and take things easy for twenty years.' That's about as simple as a plan can be, but it shows the overall shape you want your life to take. Too obvious for words? Not really; another perfectly plausible plan might be 'Make a lot of money over the next twenty years, then live in a millionaire lifestyle for the following years.' A third might be 'Lead a fulfilling life that feels complete and worthwhile.' They're all plausible and feasible (given a moderate amount of perseverance and luck for the second one), they're all simple, but they have very different implications.

You don't need to plan out the whole of the rest of your life now, nor do you need to stick to any life plan that you might choose now – you could start off planning to make a quick fortune, then realise after a couple of years that it's a pretty shallow ambition, and change instead to a life plan about developing yourself as a person; conversely, you might start off with worthy ambitions about becoming a street poet, and later decide that you'd rather lead a colourful life as an entrepreneur. It's up to you. One plan that many students find useful, if only as an excuse for postponing decisions, is to spend four or five years after university trying different things, so that they can make an informed choice, and then decide on their preferred direction after that. Why should you care about this now? Because a bit of forward planning can make a lot of difference to how easily you can reach your chosen destination. People in general, and students in particular, tend to think that exciting, cool things only happen to other people. In reality, it's surprisingly easy to do any number of exciting cool things – the reason that most people don't do them is that they simply don't try. Want to go trekking in the Himalayas? That's no more difficult to organise than a holiday in Benidorm – you start by seeing the travel agent and booking a Himalayan trekking holiday. Want to help excavate an ancient Greek archaeological site? Again, it's a case of contacting one of the relevant agencies on the Internet which will organise a place for you. Not too difficult to do, and something that you can look back on for the rest of your life.

How do you decide what you want as your long-term plan? One useful strategy is to work backwards – think about what you'd like to look back on at the end of your life, and what you'd be proud and happy to have done. Remember that good things don't only happen to other people, and that it's your life, so you can have whatever goals and ambitions you like. There's more about this in the section on job-hunting, where we discuss ways of working backwards from those goals towards the intermediate steps that move you towards them. Most people are capable of much more than they thought possible, and achieving a life's dream is a wonderful feeling. (And once you've achieved one dream, there's nothing to stop you having another if you want.) That's big-picture life planning. Plans are also useful on a smaller scale, to help you handle the average day, week, month, term and year. Stress is often caused by uncertainty; depression is often accompanied by a feeling of having no direction or purpose. A plan, even a small simple one, can help prevent these problems.

Time management

Time management, like many things in life, can sound formidable, but is based on simple principles. The idea is that you identify the things you want to do, and the time you have to do them in, and then allocate time for each task depending on how long each task is likely to take. Like budgeting, this process may reveal that you don't have enough resources (time in this case, rather than money) to complete all the tasks you would like to, in which case you may have to change what you are trying to do. The planning process itself may take up quite a bit of time at first, until you've got your system going, so allow time for that too.

Priority management

Priority management is subtly different to time management and almost every-one finds it difficult. In order to manage your priorities successfully you need to grasp two key concepts; what is Important and what is Urgent. How do you decide whether something is Important or not? Most people are really bad at this and simply respond to other people setting their deadlines for them or shouting at them. Important things affect your health your key relationships, your finances, your employment, or have a bearing on your future – such as your final year project. Urgent things may or may not be Important but have a deadline and so need to be dealt with promptly. For instance, answering a ring-ing phone may be Urgent, but when you answer and find the call is from a double-glazing salesman, you realise it isn't Important. As a rough rule-of-thumb, tasks that are both Urgent and Important need to be tackled first; then tasks which are Urgent but not Important; then Important tasks. However, you need to keep a careful eye on the Important-but-not-Urgent items because they have a tendency to become Urgent whilst you are not looking, and then you find yourself in crisis.

So, if you hear that a member of your family has been rushed to hospital following a serious accident, this is both Urgent and Important and you may need to drop everything to go and visit them. When the crisis is over, you may prioritise answering your e-mails, because they may contain some-thing Urgent and Important like a message from your tutor telling you you've missed the deadline for submitting an assignment. You respond to this e-mail first (Urgent and Important) and then the one from your mate asking you if you want tickets to see your favourite band (Urgent and of debatable Importance), then you rush over to your tutor's office clutching your assignment (Important and now Urgent).

PLANNING

Planning your planning sessions

The best way to plan your life, as we have seen, is backwards, but if you're not accustomed to thinking further ahead than the hand-in date for your next assignment, in practical terms it would be better to start planning from where you are now. First, you'll need to plan your planning sessions. A good way to start is to get out your diary or calendar (if you don't have one, then buying or making one is highly advisable). Block out a one-hour slot each week for the next month, at a time when you won't have much else on. For instance, if you find that Sunday afternoons are dull and featureless, then you can put the one-hour planning slot in then without much risk of it getting disrupted by pressure of other events. When you reach the planning slot on the first Sunday afternoon, sit down somewhere quiet and free from distractions, with a hot drink and a biscuit, if that helps. The first thing to do is to block out another date or two for future planning sessions, so that you don't get out of the habit of planning if you have to miss one session because of some unexpected event. Now you've planned your planning sessions, you can move on to short-term planning.

The next year

Start with your diary or calendar. You've already marked in some times for planning. Now mark in fixed points in the year ahead; birthdays, vacation dates, assignment deadlines, exams, gigs by your favourite bands and so on. This reduces the risk of missing something important, and therefore reduces one source of possible stress. It also gives you more of a feeling of control over your life: even if you're currently having a panic-stricken week, you now know ahead of time what you've got lined up for the following weeks, so your panic levels should reduce in future. Once you've put in your fixed points, start working backwards from each of them. For exams, think about how much time you'll need for revision and mark that period out in your diary. Do the same for assignment deadlines. And Christmas shopping. And for packing to go home for vacations. And organising the mountaineering society end-of-term party. Now you should have a pretty clear idea of what the year ahead is looking like in terms of time commitments. Look for any clashes, like the deadline for three assignments coinciding with your trip to Aberdeen for a friend's 21st. Since the trip to Aberdeen is a fixed point, set your own (earlier) deadlines for the assignments so they are finished in time. You may want to tackle them one after the other, or alongside each other, but try to set different deadlines for each. Then you can focus on the finishing touches for each of them, hopefully without panicking about the others at the same time. It may dawn on you that the three weeks before you go to Aberdeen is going to be unpleasantly pressurised, but at least you know that in advance, and that you are going to have to endure a focused period of hard slog during those three weeks, rather than the feeling of helpless panic as you set off for the station, having just e-mailed three supervisors to ask for extensions.

The next month

Now you're in a position to tackle planning for the month ahead. Check to see if anything is happening in the next month which will require you to do something now. Glasses to be ordered for the end-of-term party? Rail ticket for Aberdeen to be booked? Books to be requested from the library? Write a list and then slot the items on the list into your calendar or diary.

The next week

Next move on to weekly planning. There are various formats in which you can maintain your weekly plan. You could keep a list of things to do each day, or draw up a timetable. A timetable has the advantage of enabling you to see in advance when time is tight or when you have some free time. To save effort, you could draw up on the computer a blank template for each week and then print off a batch for the semester, to fill in each week as you go along. You'll need to update both your weekly and your monthly plan each week. The reason for this is that you'll need to keep track of things that need to be done ahead of time. Flipping over the next page of your diary on Sunday evening and realising that you've completely forgotten that you're giving a project presentation at 9am on Monday is not an enjoyable sensation, and is only marginally less uncomfortable than doing so on the Monday morning itself. Again, put in fixed points – lectures, tutorials, club meetings – first, then check your work commitments, marking in time for going over lecture notes, writing up practicals, reading set texts, ongoing assignments and so forth. You'll notice by now that your week's timetable, which started off with only three hours of commitments, is getting uncomfortably full. You've nearly got to the bit where you start to plan in free time. But first, we need to deal with contingencies.

Contingency time

As we mentioned earlier, human beings usually underestimate how long tasks are going to take, particularly tasks they haven't tackled before. The underestimate is often due to unforeseen problems arising. The more agencies (people, departments, equipment) involved in the task, the worse your estimate is likely to be, because each of the agencies is likely to experience unforeseen problems. So, if you are handwriting an essay on a topic you understand well, and are using books you've borrowed from your sister's boyfriend, chances are it will take less time than an assignment in which you have to liaise with two people in your tutor group, get books from the library, print off some complicated graphics and consult your tutor. Contingency time is the extra time you plan in to your timetable to mop up overruns. For example, you could set aside Saturday mornings for contingencies. You might not have any, in which case, you get a free Saturday morning to do with what you will. Do not be tempted to leave weekends free to catch up on any work which has not fitted in to its timetabled time. If you do, you will find you do not have much of a life. Which brings us to leisure time.

Leisure time

It may seem bizarre to include leisure time in timetabling; the reasons for doing so should soon become clear. People with very busy lives, like chief executives of blue chip companies or mothers of small children, have so many fixed points in their timetables that they have to carve out time to do things they enjoy doing. Whether it's playing golf or having a girly night out, these things are not going to happen for them spontaneously, in contrast to what happens if you are an undergraduate with a flexible timetable. People with flexible timetables tend to drift to one of two extremes; either they view all of their time as leisure time with a few irritating fixed points like lectures and panic-stricken days frantically writing assignments at the last minute, or they allow their work to dominate the timetable, and never get their act together enough for a decent day out away from work. Neither of these strategies is good for your stress levels, which is why you need to actively plan your time.

We'd got to the point where your weekly timetable was looking fuller than you'd like. It's at this point that you need to start ring-fencing free time. Using Monday-to-Friday as your basic working week is a good idea. Then you can use Saturday morning as a chance to finish off anything that needs finishing off, and that gives you the rest of the weekend free. On the other hand you may find it useful to spend Saturday or Sunday working, because then you get some uninterrupted quiet time, in which case, you would be well advised to book another day in the week as your day off. Having a big-gish chunk of leisure time has a lot of advantages over having the odd hour here and there – usually when you are feeling too exhausted or guilty to enjoy it. You can have a regular day or weekend somewhere distant, or become a key member of the archery club, or whatever. You have some time each week which you can look forward to, and you get time to unwind prop-erly. Setting aside free time like this means that people who would otherwise adopt the last-minute-panic strategy find they have more time set aside for work, and so are less likely to panic, and people who usually adopt the I've-always-got-work-hanging-over-me approach find they have guilt-free leisure time. It also means that one day a week, everybody gets a chance to remember that they are a human being.

Daily planning – the nature of time

One of the temptations open to you if you have a very flexible timetable is to assume that you can work at tasks until you've finished them, one after another, in their order of urgency. Let's imagine it's Monday morning and you have a fairly clear week, timewise, in front of you. On Friday, a mate from home will be arriving for the weekend. You have an assignment due next Monday morning, and a presentation the following Wednesday. You know the assignment will take three days, the presentation preparation one day, and you need to get some extra food and drink in for the weekend. The doing-things-in-order-of-urgency way to plan for this is to spend Monday to Wednesday working on the assignment, Thursday on the presentation, and to do shopping and hoovering on the Friday. What ends up happening is something like this: your brain is no longer working by Monday lunchtime, and Monday afternoon is spent repeatedly reading the same paragraph, so you are hugely relieved when a friend suggests going out for a drink on Monday evening. This results in you waking up just before lunch on Tuesday. You do a bit of work on Tuesday afternoon, then get a phone call from the people with whom you are doing the presentation to say that the only day they can meet you to plan is tomorrow, Wednesday, which is the day you were planning to pick up crucial books for your assignment from the library. You try to digest three books when you get back from preparing for the presentation at 10pm on Wednesday, do a bit more work on Thursday, and eventually finish the assignment at 4am on Monday after your friend has gone home.

The reason this time management strategy didn't work well is because you overlooked the fact that you are a human being. Human beings get tired and bored. If you've been doing the same kind of task for two hours or so, particularly if it's an intensive task, like reading, or working on the computer, you'll get tired and bored. Intensive reading can be very tiring indeed. Starting to read for an assignment as soon as you can has a number of advantages. It means you can do it in short chunks whenever is best for you, possibly first thing in the morning, or in the evenings. You can intersperse it with reading round other topics to break the monotony. It gives your subconscious a chance to understand and assimilate what you've read, and it gives you more flexibility for borrowing books from oversubscribed undergraduate collections. You need to go with your body on this. Your body has different kinds of time during the day, and you need to do different kinds of tasks, so if you can match the tasks to what your body feels like doing, you should get on much better. For example, most people, contrary to what it feels your body is telling you, are most alert early in the morning and in the early evening. Afternoons, biologically, tend to be siesta time. If your body works along those lines, it would be worth planning your week something like this: Work on the assignment in the mornings and evenings on Monday, Tuesday and Thursday, so you have a long break between each session. Prepare the presentation all day Wednesday, since that consists of a variety of tasks. Finish off the assignment and presentation on Friday morning, doing the hoovering as a mid-morning break. Shop on Friday afternoon. That way, your work assignments get done in a way that isn't over-taxing, and you have a free weekend with no work hanging over you. It may take a few weeks to develop a structure to your timetable which works well for you. Bear in mind that any change of routine, like the change from drifting through life to tackling it systematically and well in advance, takes time to get used to. It's worth spending a while trying different ways of working out your timetable, until you find one that feels comfortable, manageable and effective, and then allowing a couple of weeks to get used to it.

Planning for life after university: the final year project as a stepping-stone

Most students postpone planning for life after university for as long as they can, on various grounds such as (a) the world might change between now and when they graduate, (b) they have plenty of more urgent things to occupy their time, and (c) it's too scary to think about right now. That's understandable, but it tends to store up more stress for the final months of your time at university. There are various useful things you can do as far back as your second year in university which are simple, quick and often enjoyable, and which will reduce hassles in your life after university and also help your progress towards your goals.

One particularly rich area, which surprisingly few students make the most of, is the final year project. Most undergraduate courses require that final year students do a final year project or dissertation; many Master's courses have the same requirement. This is normally an individual project as opposed to group-work, and students normally have a fair amount of choice about topic. The two points of its being individual work and involving choice about topic are important ones – they give you a chance to do something distinctive and unique in an area that you like. They also give you the chance to make your project act as a stepping-stone towards where you really want to be. Suppose, for instance, you've been doing a fine art course, but you've decided that what you really want to do is to work on a wildlife reserve. Wildly different? Not necessarily. Suppose that you choose as your project topic designing and making sculptures which could be used to direct visitors in a wildlife reserve. What will this do for you? Well, for a start it will give you an excellent starting point for contacting a wildlife reserve of your choice, and offering them something for nothing (the sculptures). There's a very good chance that they'll want to co-operate with you (and even if they don't, the next reserve on your list almost certainly will). This means that by the time you graduate, they'll have been working with you for a year, and if you've given a good impression of yourself as professional, capable and pleasant to work with, there's a very good chance that they'll be thinking about offering you a job. Even if they don't, they'll be able to tell you about other jobs that are coming up elsewhere, and to give you a glowing reference.

If you're not brilliant at lateral thinking of this sort, then you'll be reassured to know that most university departments have a staff member who acts as projects co-ordinator. They're usually more than happy to talk to second year students about possible projects. Students who ask about this in their second year tend to have happy endings to their projects, which makes the co-ordinator look good; also, discussions about possible interesting projects are usually much more tempting than the admin which would otherwise be filling the co-ordinator's life. A good research project takes time, like growing a plant from seed. If you sow a small project seed in your second year, or early in your third year, then it will have plenty of time to grow into a mature plant which will produce a rich harvest when you graduate. Final year projects are one seed that's well worth sowing early. There are others. One is deciding what you'd like from your ideal job; another is to imagine your ideal life; a third is to work out what things you'd like to try at some point in your life. We describe ways of working these things out in this chapter and in the chapter on life after university. These strategies can give you useful and fascinating insights into yourself. The outcomes can also help you identify information gaps, so you can start finding out more about relevant topics, such as what will improve your chances of getting a particular job.

Long-term planning

Once you've mastered the art of planning your days, weeks, months and years, it can be helpful to set aside a day, or part of a day, each year to check that your long-term plans are on track. If you don't, you'll keep putting it off until you suddenly find that five years has passed and you haven't even started to think about where the recent drastic changes in your life are taking you. One of us used to use New Year's Day to do long-term planning, as a quiet time without interruptions, until over-exuberant New Year's Eve celebrations began to interfere with the tradition. Summer holidays can also be a good time for reflection on where you are going and where you want to be. It may be helpful to find a 'buddy' to do this with you, so you can bounce your ideas off each other. Go somewhere you like, but somewhere not too distracting, where you can let ideas flow without interruption – Eastbourne rather than Alton Towers. You might not need to change your plans at all, but at least you'll have a good day out with a mate. Long-term planning, however fanciful it seems at the time, can have a very therapeutic effect if you are feeling overwhelmed by short-term issues; it gets things in perspective and encourages you to think of other pathways for your life.

By now a pattern for planning should be apparent. The longer the time-span you're planning for, the fuzzier your planning is going to be, because the further ahead you're thinking, the less information you're going to have about the situation you'll be in. Your plan for the next fifty years may contain vague ideas about getting married and becoming a millionaire; your plan for the next hour may include six very specific things you need do before going to a lecture. It's helpful to organize your time planning in different timeframes; you might have lifetime, ten-year, five-year, one-year, one-month, oneweek and daily timeframes, for example. The lifetime timeframe will only need to be revisited occasionally, probably when your life takes a dramatically different course, such as your unexpectedly being approached with the offer of a PhD when you were planning to become a market gardener. The ten-year and five-year timeframes will need to be reconsidered, say, once a year, the annual plan once a month, the monthly plan once a week and the weekly and the daily timeframe will need to be updated daily.

Planning as a way to reduce stress

We've identified a number of ways in which planning can help you take control of your life. Another way is that you can identify things that are causing you hassle, and put in some strategies for handling them. For instance, if the campus shops don't give you much choice in food or stationery or music, then you can plan in a session with Yellow Pages or the Internet to identify some specialist suppliers, and then plan an expedition for some bulk buying, or a session doing some online shopping. If you find evenings boring and bleak, then plan in some evening activities other than going to the union bar – you could probably find a different university society for every week of the year, even without counting entertainment on offer locally, hobbies or simply reading a good book. If you're overloaded with work, then plan in an hour of quiet time each week for relaxing, with no work allowed. If you think that you can't spare an hour for this, then try some mental arithmetic – an hour a week works out to about nine minutes a day, and if you can't carve out this much time, you're probably doing too much and need to consult your personal tutor. In practice, taking some time out from the work will almost certainly help you to see things more in perspective, and to work more efficiently, which will save you more time in the long run as well as making you feel better.

This is a good point at which to recall two of the concepts mentioned at the start of this book. One is artificial ecstasy as opposed to natural ecstasy; the other is instrumental behaviour as opposed to expressive behaviour. It's worth looking at your goals, and asking whether they're just a larger than usual dose of artificial ecstasy, to take your mind off the unpleasant realities of your everyday life; if so, it would be wise to think about goals that will make your day-to-day reality positively enjoyable. It's also worth considering whether your approach to your goals is instrumental, where you set out some goals and then work out ways of achieving them, or expressive, where you set out some goals to show people what sort of person you are, but without any serious intention to do anything about making them happen.

SUMMARY

Life planning helps you to make the most of your time, and to achieve your goals and dreams. Some simple strategies can help you to identify the things you really want out of life, and help you to achieve them. One good strategy is to imagine yourself looking back from old age on the things that you've done; what would you want to look back on?

BIBLIOGRAPHY AND SUGGESTED FURTHER RESOURCES

The Tiny Book of Time: Creating Time for the Things that Matter by K. Pickin and N. Singer (Headline, 1999) does what its title says; gives you a lot of wise advice in bite-sized chunks about managing your time to support what matters to you. It's also tiny, so it's easy to keep in a pocket or handbag as a source of inspiration if you need some positive thoughts near to hand during the day.

Living the 80/20 way: Work Less, Worry Less, Succeed More, Enjoy More by Richard Koch (Nicholas Brealey Publishing, 2004) is a good example of how to apply the Pareto distribution to your planning.

If the standard principles of time management seem too constricting, over-structured and detailed you may find *Organizing for the Creative Person* by D. Lehmkuhl and D.C. Lamping (Three Rivers Press, 1993) more useful and on your wavelength.

9

Aftermath

(or, Is there life after university, and is it really scary?)

> The big picture. Job-hunting. Deciding what you want to do with your life. Job applications. Job interviews. The first week at work. Forward planning while at university. Gap years, sandwich years and mature students.

Life after university in general, and finding a job in particular, can be a major source of stress for students during the final year at university. The underlying reasons for the stress are the usual suspects, such as:

- Uncertainty ('What options are open to me? What will I end up doing?')
- Control ('Will I get the job I apply for?')
- Dread ('What if I don't manage to find anything, and end up with a dog on a string, living on the streets?')

As usual, there are things that you can do about all of these fears; as usual, these things include planning and preparation, your old friends the de-stressing exercises, and ways of learning and moving on if everything goes awry. The next sections describe the stages of job-finding in broadly chronological order, though we've also covered longer-term life planning both in the first section (since you'll need to take this into account when deciding which types of job to go for) and in the last section (since you'll need to take stock of your life periodically after leaving university). Before we get into those topics, there's one important piece of advice you might find useful if you've come straight from school to university. Most students in this position view the outside world as a scary place of cut-throat competition and the grim rat-race of corporate industry, apart from a few incredibly cool jobs which only a rare few are lucky or manipulative enough to get. It's rarely like that; most workplaces are populated by ordinary human beings who are accustomed to human shortcomings, especially in inexperienced new graduates. Most people sooner or later move into a job that suits them, and work there happily for years, making friendships that usually last longer than the jobs, and in many cases finding lovers and partners there. So, with that bit of reassurance given, how do you set about finding the right job and life for yourself? We'll start with job-hunting.

JOB-HUNTING

The traditional approach

There is a traditional approach to job-hunting which is widely used by final year students, and which is a rich source of stress. It goes as follows. First, worry your head off about final year exams. Second, put off looking for a job until the last possible moment because you're focusing on final year exams. Third, try to do your job-hunting at the same time as taking your final year exams. Finally, worry during the exams about whether you're going to be unemployed after graduating. It's traditional, and it's widespread, but so are toothache and hangovers; after that cheering introduction, you might be glad to know that job-hunting needn't be particularly stressful. What you can do is as follows.

The effective approach

A useful strategy for tackling things that you find a bit scary is to imagine how you'd tackle something similar which isn't scary. So, if you're nervous about the thought of tracking down a job, you could instead think about how you'd track down a wild animal and take a photo of it for your album. We'll work through this process briefly, and then go into more detail about how to apply each step to job-hunting. First of all, which sort of animal would you want to photograph? It's up to you. You might want to go for a dormouse or a moose or a whale; there aren't any right or wrong answers. Obvious? It is in relation to photographing animals, but it's easy to miss this point when deciding what sort of job to go for. There's a widespread assumption that you have to go for a high-status white-collar job. That isn't so; it's your life, and it's up to you to decide what you want to do with it. If, like one of our students, you want to work in a wildlife sanctuary, then that's fine; you don't need to become a manager. If you go for what you really want, then you're much less likely to be stressed, and much more likely to be happy and fulfilled. How do you work out what you really want, if you don't already know this? There's a section on that coming up. In the meantime, back to the photography project.

Next, you need to work out what's involved in taking the photo: where do you need to be, and when; what sort of kit do you need, and so on? If you're planning to photograph a grizzly bear in the wild, then you'll need to travel to North America, and you'll need to know where bears are particularly likely to be at what times of the year and what times of the day; it will also be advisable to learn about using telephoto lenses and about how to avoid antagonising bears. If you're applying for a particular job, or type of job, then you need to know where to find out about it, and what you'll need to have on your CV, and how to apply in a way that won't deter the prospective employer.

Finally, you need to get out there and take the photo. Do you expect to get a brilliant photo immediately? Obviously not; it might take a long time to get the photograph that you really want. It depends on your needs. If you want to take a snapshot of a bear just so you can say you've done it, then you can probably get an adequate picture pretty quickly. If you want an amazing photograph that will inspire you for the rest of your life, then that will take longer, and will take practice. Similarly with jobs. You can't know for sure what sort of job you'll really like until you've tried it; usually your first job or two are part of the learning process, helping you work out what you really want to do with your life, and doing what is needed to get you to that destination. Even after you've found something that makes you really happy, you might decide a few years later that you want to move on to something else; that's all part of life as a process that goes on throughout your time on this planet.

If you tackle job-hunting in this way, you should end up with more knowledge about the situation (reducing uncertainty and therefore reducing stress) and more control of the situation (reducing any stress due to lack of control). It should also help you produce contingency plans for what to do next (reducing stress by giving you more certainty and more control). How do you set about working out your strategy for getting the job you really want? Here are some ideas.

DECIDING WHAT YOU WANT TO DO WITH YOUR LIFE

Work backwards
Imagine that the wise, contented elderly you is looking back on your life. What would you want to look back on? What would you want to have done before you died? What would you be proud of?

Work forwards from job advertisements
Get a batch of job adverts, including ones that you know you'd hate and ones that you aren't qualified for yet. Go through them with two highlighters, using one colour for job features that turn you off, and the other colour for job features that you really like. Draw up a list of the negative and

the positive features, and write some notes to yourself explaining why you like or dislike each feature. This gives you a description of what your ideal job would be like. You can then take this description to career advisers, friends, parents of friends, lecturers and others, and ask them if they know any jobs that fit that description. There's a good chance that someone will; even if you don't get the ideal job immediately, you'll at least have something realistic to work towards.

Working out where to be and what you need

Most students look for jobs in newspapers and magazines. This works to some extent, but it's not a very efficient strategy. You end up competing with huge numbers of other students who are reading the same sources, and you'll be applying as just another applicant. There are better strategies. Most students also base their application on the expected class and topic of their degree, and any extra things that they happen to be able to think of, such as society memberships. Again, there are better ways. An excellent source of advice on this and related topics is the book *What Color is Your Parachute?* by Richard Bolles; it's updated regularly, and is in most libraries. It's American, and therefore sometimes irrelevant to British readers, and it has some strong Christian messages in places, but the vast majority of it is solid, practical advice which is relevant to job-hunters everywhere. Here are some strategies you may find useful for keeping control and reducing uncertainty.

Apply warm, not cold

If an employer already knows you, and thinks you're good, then (a) they'll probably let you know when a job is coming up and (b) you'll have a better chance of getting that job, since you're a known quantity. Note that this is emphatically not the same as using the old school tie network (where you manage to land a job because of who you know, rather than on merit) – we disapprove strongly of unfair practices of that sort. Applying warm means that the employer gets to know you because of what you've done with them, not because of who you or your parents went to school with. A good way of applying warm is to do a final year project which brings you into contact with a potential employer, or to do a summer job with them.

Do some homework

Most applicants don't bother to find out much about the organisation they're applying to spend the next few years working for. Applicants who do some homework have a much better chance of being offered a job.

Look in the specialist press

Adverts in the broadsheet newspapers (for example the *Guardian*, *The Times*, the *Independent* and the *Daily Telegraph*) typically attract huge numbers of applicants. Adverts in local papers are often for low-level jobs. The specialist press (for example professional advertising magazines if you want a job in advertising) contain many advertisements for jobs that don't appear anywhere else, and which are likely to give you a much better hit rate.

Get relevant skills and experience onto your CV

Many employers ask for a degree and previous experience, which is a frequent source of complaints about unfairness – how can you get experience without getting the job in the first place? You can do something about this if you start well in advance – it takes time. You can often get relevant experience via summer jobs, or via unpaid voluntary work for a good cause, or via your final year project. It's not the same as a year's full-time experience, but it shows initiative, and that goes down well with prospective employers. You'll probably have to do a summer job and/or a final year project anyway, so it's no extra effort to select ones that support your overall CV.

JOB APPLICATIONS

Most of the process of applying for jobs is usually a hassle rather than actively stressful; we'll work through that in a moment. One part which almost everyone does find stressful, though, is the thought of being rejected by a potential employer, so we'll tackle that first. Job applications are like many other things in life: a key principle is to choose your calibration level. Expecting to be offered interviews for every single job you apply for is clearly silly; even if you did achieve this, it would simply mean that you were aiming too low, and would have a realistic chance of getting a significantly better job if you tried. Similarly, expecting not to be offered interviews for any of the jobs you apply for would be silly, and achieving this rate would mean that either you were pitching your applications too high, or that you were doing something wrong with your applications, which would need to be identified and fixed. A success rate somewhere between these extremes tells you that you're being realistic in your ambitions and that you're putting the applications together reasonably well. It's up to you to decide what rate you consider appropriate; most people consider something between a 10 per cent and a 25 per cent hit rate to be about right. Once you've done this, the letters become useful calibration points rather than signalling personal rejection.

You can improve your hit rate, and reduce hassles, by a few simple strategies.

- Start looking and applying early.
- Budget a reasonable amount of time – measure how long the first application takes you, and allow the same amount for each subsequent application so you don't rush them and make needless mistakes.

- Find out about how to write really good applications; ask someone knowledgeable for advice. There's a lot of information available, and you should make yourself familiar with it – it's helping move you towards where you want to be.
- Pay attention to detail in your applications.
- Plan a reward for yourself after each application, and make sure to enjoy that reward.
- If your hit rate is significantly below what you expected, take advice from someone knowledgeable and helpful – it's likely to be due to something simple and fixable.
- Don't be tempted to resort to expressive behaviour (see Chapter 1). Having completed a hundred unsuccessful job applications doesn't show people how determined you are to get a job; it shows you are someone who is applying for the wrong jobs or applying in the wrong way.

JOB INTERVIEWS

Job interviews are a classic source of stress and needless pain. One effective strategy is, again, simply to draw up a list of the things that you're worried about. Most of these will probably derive from not knowing something, in which case the obvious solution is to find out the answer, rather than agonising about uncertainty. To save you time this section deals with some of the classic questions. There's a lot of information available about how to do job interviews, and it's well worth reading up on this.

When the letter arrives

When you are invited to an interview, reply to confirm that you'll be attending. If you can't make that date and time, then ask politely whether they can offer another time. If they can't, thank them politely – there's a good chance that they'll then remember you favourably next time they have a job going.

Before the interview

- Check that your interview clothes are clean and tidy. If you don't have any interview clothes, get some. Err on the side of discreet smartness. Make sure your shoes are clean (yes, a lot of employers pay attention to that; if you've skimped on shoe-cleaning, what else might you skimp on if they employ you?). Make sure you're comfortable wearing the interview clothes, so you don't fidget on the day.
- Check that you know how to get to the interview with plenty of time to spare, so you're not rushing and stressed. Take travel details with you, plus spare cash in case of last-minute emergencies.

- Read the 'information for candidates' documents carefully; doing this on the train can be a useful stress-reduction activity.
- If possible, have a practice interview with someone who's used to interviewing job applicants, and who's willing to give you feedback. If possible, video record the practice interview and view it afterwards. This can make an enormous difference to your success rate. Show appreciation to this person – even if their advice contains unwelcome home truths, it's giving you a chance to change your life greatly for the better.
- On arrival, let the relevant person know that you've arrived. Freshen up, in case your hair has been blown around by the wind on the way in, or something else has gone askew.

You'll probably be asked to wait somewhere until the time of your interview. Most people find the waiting stressful. You can handle this in various ways:

- *Relaxation and centring exercises*, as described in Chapter 2 and in the appendices. Calm breathing, with your favourite relaxation images, will put you in a much better frame of mind.
- *Use the time to take control* by mentally rehearsing points you want to make, and questions you want to ask the interviewers.
- *Re-read the background information* about the job and the organisation.
- *Think about what you've learned since walking through the door* – does this give the impression of being a happy organisation which will be a good place to work in, or a miserable grim place that you want to leave as soon as possible?
- *Think about the plan B that you prepared previously*, for what you'll do if you don't get this job. That will help keep this job in focus, so you don't become fixated with trying to get it at all costs.

During the interview

Most people find job interviews stressful because they perceive themselves as being tested in a context where they don't have all the relevant information and where they don't have control. This is partly true, but if you take a different perspective, then the situation becomes rather different. The interview is a two-way interaction, where you and the potential employer find out about each other and decide whether or not you would like to work with each other. Because time is limited, neither you nor they will be able to say absolutely everything that's relevant, so you'll both be in the dark to some extent. However, you can use the interview to gather the main information that you need to make your decision (apart from salary, which is usually discussed only after they've made you an offer). The three golden principles for situations of this sort are simple:

- don't lie
- don't try to be funny
- don't panic and blurt out the truth.

Although this advice looks humorous, it's actually extremely practical. You shouldn't say anything you know to be untrue; that's unethical, and at a practical level, there's a good chance you'll be found out and chucked out. You should treat the interview and the interviewers with due courtesy; it's not a place to show off and make wisecracks. (Some people react to stress by joking; that's fine in some contexts, but not here.) The last bit of advice is the subtlest and the most important; you're allowed and expected to gild the lily and put a favourable gloss on things that you've done, provided that there is a lily in the first place and that you've actually done those things. If you needlessly blurt out the embarrassing reality beneath the gilding when there's no reason for doing so, then it doesn't reflect well on your judgement – would you blurt out similarly embarrassing things in front of a client if you were hired?

Walk into the interview room with head up and shoulders back; it helps your posture and your feeling of self-esteem. Smile and say hello to the interviewers; shake hands if they appear to expect it, then take a seat when they offer it. They'll probably start with a harmless question to put you at ease, such as how your journey was; a simple 'Fine, thanks' with a smile is enough to handle this and to show them that you're calm and courteous.

Their task now is to find out how well you're likely to fit with the job. Some of the questions they ask might sound odd; this is often because they've had to ask a previous candidate about some oddity in their application, and they're now asking all the other candidates the same in the interests of fairness and consistency. If you're not sure what a question means, then you can simply ask politely for clarification. There are some classic questions that you can expect, and which are listed in most of the texts about job interview technique, such as 'What attracted you to this job?' You should have answers ready for these questions; they're one of the bits of preparation that you do long before the interview. One very useful tip is to read a couple of books written for job interviewers (as opposed to interviewees), which will give you more understanding of the process from the interviewers' perspective. When answering the questions, it's wise to stick to demonstrable facts rather than opinion about yourself wherever possible. It's also wise to have a mental list of points you want to get into your replies somewhere, and to do what you can to create opportunities to get those points made – the interviewers' questions won't always uncover things such as unusual achievements during your gap year. Usually it's possible to get these points in early, when they ask you why you think you're a good candidate for this job, and again at the end, when they ask if there are any other points you'd like to make. If you go blank, then it's permissible to smile, apologise and explain that you've gone blank, then ask them to repeat the question. They'll be used to this happening with other interviewees, and will almost certainly be reasonable. If they aren't, then you have the option of choosing not to work with them if they offer you the job; that's under your control. At the end of the interview, thank them, smile and leave.

After the interview

If you get a letter of rejection, then add it to your calibration list, and see how you're doing. Use your reassurance strategy (whatever consolation treat you've lined up for yourself). We find it effective to wallow in self-pity in any spare moments for the rest of the day, eat some comfort food and watch a cathartic movie in the evening, to get the emotions out of our systems; the next day, we expect to bounce back and ask ourselves what we can learn from the experience. Sometimes you know that you screwed up, and you can work out or find out how not to make that mistake again. Other times you didn't screw up, and the interviewers had the difficult problem of choosing between four candidates who were all completely appointable, with hardly any difference between them. In that situation, there's no shame in not being offered the job, and they might well ask you to apply for other jobs in the future. Sometimes you screw up without realising it; if you're getting a pattern of rejection letters for no reason that makes sense to you, then you can try phoning the organisation and asking politely whether they can give you any feedback. Sometimes the answer is yes, and sometimes it's no, but it's worth a polite try. (Anger, or trying to argue with their reasoning, is inadvisable; it's unprofessional in this context, and it wipes out your prospects of being asked to apply for the next job they're advertising.)

What happens if they offer you the job? Remember that you don't need to accept it. It's perfectly reasonable to ask for a short amount of time – for instance, a day or two – to think it over. Some polite phrasing is a good idea (for instance, 'It looks really interesting, but in some ways it wasn't what I was expecting; could I have a day to think it over?') This buys you some thinking time, and a chance to take advice.

THE FIRST WEEK AT WORK

When you get a job, the first week at work shouldn't bring too many new challenges in terms of stress; just things that you already know how to handle. It's in your employer's interests to make sure that you're given the right information to get started, though in practice you may not get as much information as you'd like. You can prevent or reduce some classic potential stressors via the usual strategy of listing the things you're worrying about, and then working out how you're going to handle each one. For instance, if you're worried about being late for work on your first day, then work out a schedule that gives you plenty of time; if there's anything particularly problematic, then you can try strategies such as a practice journey to the workplace on a day before you start work, or asking a friend for help. If there's something about the workplace that you don't know and that is worrying you, then you can usually phone up and check before you start.

A few basic strategies will prevent or reduce most potential stressors during the first week.

- Be punctual, both for starting work and for meetings at work.
- If in doubt about what you're supposed to be doing, ask your line manager
- Don't mess about, even if other people are doing so. You're new, and haven't earned the right to bend the rules.
- Err on the side of dressing smartly but inconspicuously.
- Err on the side of keeping quiet during the first week.
- Pay attention to detail, and work cleanly and neatly.

It's wise to observe the longer-serving staff — do they look cheerful and happy with their work, or do they look oppressed and miserable? If they're miserable, then that's probably what will happen to you if you stay there too long. If they're happy, then any problems you might hit in the first week are likely to be temporary ones. Either way, it's a good idea not to bail out of an organisation within a few weeks of starting – that looks bad on the CV, suggesting that you don't have any staying power. The only exception is if the organisation is doing something illegal, in which case you should get out as soon as possible, but that situation is fortunately rare. The usual rule of thumb among prospective employers is that if someone makes a habit of leaving a job in less than two years, that could signal a problem (note: 'makes a habit' as opposed to 'occasionally' – you don't need to do exactly two years minimum in every job). It's also a good idea to have a moderately firm game plan for the next couple of years, and then a fuzzier one for the few years after that, which you update periodically; this strikes a balance between being a rudderless jellyfish on the sea of fate, and being an obsessive control freak who tries to plan every detail of their life for the next forty years.

GAP YEARS, SANDWICH YEARS AND MATURE STUDENTS

Gap years and sandwich years both offer some obvious advantages in relation to job-hunting and career planning – they give you experience that can go on the CV, they give you contacts and they give you personal first-hand experience of what a particular type of work is like. All of these factors can reduce the potential for stress.

Mature students often face another set of potential stressors and depressors when it comes to job-hunting, if they are using their degree to help them move into a new type of work. These are usually worries and obsessive thoughts along the lines of 'I'm too old and therefore too expensive; I can't compete with 21-year-old graduates.' A bit of calibration should help put this in perspective. What percentage of organisations will want to hire only young graduates for all their jobs, including senior management jobs? The figure of zero comes to mind. A more fruitful and realistic question is to ask about what sort of post would require someone with considerable experience in one field and a degree in another field. That gives you a much more realistic goal to aim for. If you're a mature student, it's usually a mistake to go for the sort of jobs that the 21-year-olds are going for; it's wiser to capitalise on your previous experience. Whatever you've done, even if it's something that unkind people joke about, like being a hairdresser or a housewife, you've got proven experience. If a job interviewer asks you whether you can handle multi-tasking, you can tell them that you can cook dinner while keeping two toddlers out of mischief – anyone senior enough to be interviewing job applicants will probably understand very well what's involved in that bit of multi-tasking. One strategy that you might find useful is to aim your first applications after you've completed your degree at jobs that are similar to the ones you did prior to university, so you can draw directly on some of that experience. For instance, if you're a former librarian, and have just completed a music degree with a view to working in a recording studio, you might not be able to do so without experience in the music industry. However, you could start by applying for jobs involving music archiving, or cataloguing, where you may have a better chance of getting employment because of your previous experience in libraries. Once you've got that first job, you should then find it easier to move sideways into record production, taking things at your own pace.

Case study from Susie: Carolyn had, to her surprise, inherited enough money to retire at a fairly young age. She was also surprised to find, as with any sudden unexpected change, her welcome windfall proved to be a very stressful event. She had no idea of her purpose in life and had not really ever thought about planning beyond getting a job and getting married. The money turned into a source of stress and in her first counselling session the phrase 'But what will I *do*?' was repeated and repeated. Like many students, she had focused only on her career and work and she needed help to look at her life from a broader perspective. Thinking about her life as a whole helped her to see the money as an opportunity and a source of joy, rather than a burden.

SUMMARY

Some forward planning can make the transition from university to the outside world much easier and can move you much closer to where you want to be. Doing some homework about the places where you're applying for jobs, and practising interview skills, will significantly improve your chances of getting the job you want. Having said that, there's more to life than work; it's important to work out what you want from life, and where your work fits into that bigger picture, so you have a balanced life that brings you contentment. You can prevent or reduce many potential stressors by doing some forward planning, including:

- making contact with potential employers well before graduating – for instance, via a summer job or your final year project
- reading up on job-hunting, job applications, interview technique, and related topics
- working out what sort of job you want to do in the longer term, and what sort of jobs you're willing to do in the shorter term as a route to the longer term
- working out a plan B
- asking someone helpful and knowledgeable to give you some feedback on your application letters, CV and interview technique.

BIBLIOGRAPHY AND SUGGESTED FURTHER RESOURCES

R.N. Bolles's *What Color Is Your Parachute?: A Practical Manual for Job-hunters and Career-changers* (Ten Speed Press), is updated regularly and is a classic, with a lot of excellent advice about taking charge of your career and your life. At time of writing, there was also an excellent supporting website with further material – a search on 'Bolles' and 'parachute' should find it.

For help in working out your purpose in life, you might find some of the life-coaching literature useful. An example is Fiona Harrold's *The 10-Minute Life Coach: Fast Working Strategies for a New You* (Hodder & Stoughton, 2002), which has a section devoted to 'where are you going?'

Martin Seligman's book *Authentic Happiness: Using the New Positive Psychology to Realize Your Potential for Lasting Fulfillment* (Free Press, 2004) introduces Positive Psychology and includes practical advice to help cultivate optimism and happiness. We've mentioned it before, but it's worth re-mentioning it here.

10

The forgotten army: mature, part-time and overseas students

(or, Does anyone ever think about us?)

> Feeling as if you don't fit in: before you start; mature students; juggling responsibilities at home and university. Part-time students: work–life balance. Issues affecting students from overseas. Other students from minority groups.

If you're a part-time student, a mature student or a student from overseas, then there's a small word which you're likely to hear quite often when you deal with the university system. It's 'Ah.' You'll often hear it when you ask an administrator what the situation is for part-time, mature or overseas students; it usually means either 'Damn, we forgot about them when we wrote that set of regulations' or 'Damn, I'll have to dig out the regulations about this.' That's a bit better than 'Ha, this regulation will make them unhappy', but not much better in practical terms. If you're in one of these categories, or a similar one such as year-abroad students and sandwich-year students, then The System is likely to overlook you in ways that bring hassle and stress to your life.

As people who have been part-time, mature and year-abroad students in our time, we know what it's like to go through this, and we sympathise with anyone who's sharing that experience. There are some exceptions. Some universities specialise in part-time courses, often aimed at mature students, and do an excellent job with them, as we can testify from personal experience; some specialise in courses designed for overseas students, and do these so well that the overseas students stay in touch with the university even decades later, when they're government ministers back in their home country, as we can testify from knowing some of those happy students. However, the majority of undergraduate courses at British universities are based on an implicit simplifying assumption that all the students will be full-time, home-grown and straight from school. When a course is run both in full-time mode and also in part-time mode, then there is a tendency for the part-time version to be overlooked. This isn't done out of malice, prejudice or ignorance; it's simply a reflection of the time pressures put on British academics these days. The result is that you are likely to hit two main problems, and various minor problems.

FEELING AS IF YOU DON'T FIT IN

Lack of regulations

You will probably find sooner or later that the university's regulations either don't say anything about an issue which is affecting you, or that the university's regulations are inconsistent. For instance, if you are a part-time student and your company suddenly decides to send you to Switzerland for three months, there may not be any regulations covering this situation. Alternatively, there may be one regulation about being sent away on company business, and another regulation about absences of up to six months, and these may contradict each other. If this happens, then you're going to feel understandably angry or otherwise upset. If you're in this situation, do some of the calming exercises in Chapter 2 and in the appendices, then think through the situation in terms of what outcome you want, and how best to get there, including which information you'll need to find out. Sometimes an emotional scene will produce the short-term result you want, but that comes with a price, in terms of how other people perceive you – not many people want to work with someone who becomes emotional whenever there's a problem, so it's inadvisable to use the emotional scene except as a last resort. A more effective strategy is usually to write a clear letter or email explaining the situation, quoting the relevant regulations, and asking the relevant person to tell you what you should do. This turns the situation from your problem into their problem, so you can get on with your life while they decide what to do. A useful addition to this strategy is to ask them whether you should do X or Y, where both X and Y are options that you'd be happy with. This tactic is usually worth a try – it doesn't challenge the decision-maker's authority, and it gives them a simple, clearly defined menu of options if they're overworked and rushed (which they usually are). There's a chance that they'll go for one of these options rather than spending a cheerless couple of hours wading through the regulations in case there's an option Z that you haven't mentioned. This doesn't always work – some bureaucrats know the relevant regulations without needing to re-read the documentation, and sometimes the options you've identified are actually storing up potential trouble for you later on – but it's worth having it in your repertoire.

Feeling marginalised

You will almost certainly feel marginalised at some point in your studies – you will get the impression that the university doesn't care about you, and is only interested in the money that you pay it in fees. It's an understandable feeling. However, that doesn't mean it's necessarily true. Most students feel marginalised sooner or later for one reason or another. First year undergraduates feel that lecturers view them as an anonymous mob, of little interest compared to second and third years. Final year students feel that the university doesn't pay enough attention to them in terms of support, such as making the first and second years keep quiet when it's revision time and the final exams are looming. If you ever end up working in a large organisation with responsibility for a number of people, then you'll soon discover that even the most caring organisations often give the impression of marginalising people for the simple reason that everyone is just too busy to think of all the human issues all the time. It's nothing personal. This may not sound very encouraging initially. However, there is one way in which it is very useful information, in relation to stress. The thing to remember is that if you are feeling stressed, miserable and lonely, then it's probably because The System is badly set up, not because there's something wrong with you. That may appear cold comfort when you're going through a bad time, but it's actually quite constructive, since it means that you probably don't need to contemplate a session of confronting your own shortcomings in addition to handling the immediate problem – you just need to work out how to live with The System. The following sections describe some of those areas where The System can cause you problems, and what you can do about them. We begin with a section on issues that affect more or less everyone. There's then a section for mature students, another for students on part-time courses, a third for students from overseas, and a fourth for students in categories other than those just mentioned.

BEFORE YOU BEGIN

This section begins with the question of whether doing a degree is the right choice for you at this time in your life; sometimes it's better to do so while you have the chance, but sometimes it's better to wait until a time that's better for you. The following sections work through preparations that you can make to give yourself more support during your time as a student, then some common stressors affecting the readers for whom this chapter is intended, and finally a section on what to do if the degree doesn't feel like the right thing for you.

Is a degree the right thing for you at this point?

It takes considerable commitment and good time management to follow a degree course; to do so whilst holding down a job or looking after a young family takes great commitment and excellent time management; to do so whilst holding down a job *and* looking after a family takes the steely resolve and organisational skills of a nursing sister in a First World War field hospital. That's the bad news. The good news is that most students who go through this emerge feeling glad that they did it, and with good memories of their times on the course. After that reassurance, if you're in one of the categories above, then it's still wise to ask yourself right at the start whether this is the best time for you to be doing a degree. It may sound like a good idea in terms of enhanced career prospects and income, but the cost in terms of employer's goodwill and family relationships may be very high. However, don't assume it would be better to wait until your children are older or you're in a more senior job. Ironically, it's sometimes easier to take a degree when children are young. You are more likely to find someone who will entertain a couple of toddlers for an hour or two than to be able to find someone willing to explain to your child's school and the local constabulary how your teenager happened to be purloining goods from a shop when they were supposed to be in school, particularly when the teenager blames the crime on having a parent who is too busy studying to look after them properly.

Some things to check before you make your final decision to do the course

If you're planning to do the course while employed, then make sure your employer is aware of precisely what time commitment your course of study actually involves. This will have the added advantage of making *you* aware of what time commitment your course of study actually involves. Employers often like the idea of an employee engaging in a course of study; they end up with a better qualified employee at little or no cost to themselves and it can enhance their reputation as a company which empowers its workers. But you can be sure that, when faced with a choice between sending you to a vital European sales conference and allowing you a day's annual leave to finish an assignment, it is unlikely that the assignment will win. If you're in this situation then it's worth building up as much goodwill as you can before you start the course. If you're one of those valued people who covered for absent colleagues and came in for the weekend to move furniture during an office relocation, your application for support when studying will probably be viewed more favourably than if you have a reputation as an unhelpful clock-watcher.

Some employers already have formal arrangements in place for employees who are studying. Sometimes this is a good thing. It at least means you are likely to be allowed time to study. But you will need to check that the arrangements you need are the ones that the employer is offering. If the arrangements are based on what Engineering requested for Phil and Dave, who both needed to spend three months gathering data in the Far East, that may not fit in very well with your requirements for covering your English Literature modules at the Open University. If you can get your employer to agree to a sabbatical, or to a part-time contract whilst you complete the course, and you can afford to take a drop in salary, so much the better. Your stress levels will probably come within the normal range if you can do so.

WHEN YOU START

Support networks

Assuming that you have decided to go ahead with becoming a student, then the next step is to make sure that you have an adequate support network. The more relatives, friends and work colleagues you can rope into babysitting, running errands and covering for you at work, the better. Let your tutors and lecturers know as early as possible that you have work and family commitments, especially if you are a primary carer. Don't expect special treatment, since university staff are obliged to assess your work on the same criteria as all other students, but it will improve the chances of their being flexible when any problems crop up, particularly in relation to deadlines and emergencies.

Time-planning

If you're taking a degree course whilst working, or looking after a family, the chances are you have already done some long-term planning. You will need to keep reassessing your progress and your long-term plans from time to time, but your real challenge is going to be effective time and priority management in the short-term. Planning the year ahead is going to be much the same for you as for full-time students with no other commitments, except that you are going to have much less study time available (see Chapter 8). With regard to short-term planning, you will be in a very different situation to full-time students. You're not going to have the luxury of being able to tackle tasks one after the other, in order of urgency. It's probably just as well, because, unless your course involves a lot of practical work, you are better off dividing the work into chunks anyway, and leaving time for refreshment and reflection between tasks. It's tempting to carve out long periods like entire weekends or two weeks' leave in a writers' retreat in which to work. Resist this temptation unless you are sure that this is what you need, which it may be if you're tackling a lengthy piece of written work that requires complex coherent thought. An hour or two of study first thing in the morning before you go to work, an hour at lunchtime and a couple of hours in the evening after the kids have gone to bed, gives you five hours study time a day, which is more than most mortals can cope with. If you have a long drive to work, consider using public transport instead, so you can work whilst you travel. Commuter trains offer ample opportunity for study – you may be crammed in like cattle en route to the abattoir, but you'll be crammed in with people reading newspapers, catching up on paperwork, writing novels and preparing presentations, who take a dim view of those who want to share their taste in music or their telephone conversations with their neighbours, so there may be comparatively little distraction.

Priority management

This is different to time-management and almost everyone finds it difficult. It is a common problem for people working in matrix organisations, who have more than one immediate boss, or for students who are working and who have families, since you can find yourself in situations where each of the domains you operate in has thrown something at you that needs to be done urgently. There are various techniques to help with priority management, which you can find on pages 27–28. Ask yourself questions about the task you have to prioritise. First *is blood involved?* Is there a health and safety issue? Second; *how important is it?* What are the consequences if I don't do it? Third; *how urgent is it?* If your child is rushed to hospital or your father has had a heart attack, then this takes priority over everything else. You may need to prioritise an important issue, such as getting your central heating fixed, over an urgent issue like meeting an assignment deadline.

Delegating responsibility

Going back to the previous example about priority management, don't assume that you are the only person who can look after your child or your father. Delegate that task to others if you can, once the initial emergency is over. Similarly in everyday life, it's often possible to delegate tasks such as tending the baby or undertaking the school run to your partner (allow a few weeks to get the routine running smoothly) or to a friend or relative, so you have some study time before you leave for work. You could try arriving at work early, or leaving late, so that you can study when the office is empty. Assignments can be completed effectively with carefully arranged support from a long-suffering partner and a network of friends and relations.

Motivation

Take one step at a time. Clichéd advice, but sound. You are not tackling an entire degree course at once, and by the time you are in your final year, your family circumstances and your work situation could have changed dramatically. Something that seems like an insurmountable obstacle now may not be an issue in a month's time. Plan ahead, but aim to get through one task, then another. Reward yourself when you complete each task. Exercise is an ally. You may be able to set aside time for a morning jog, or an evening or two at the gym each week, but a brisk walk round the park, or a regular stint in the garden are probably more realistic for most people. Activities like these not only compensate for a sedentary lifestyle, they also give you the opportunity to assimilate and reflect on your coursework, often at a subconscious level, where you can start to grasp the deep structure of your field of study.

If it's all too much

It's not the end of the world if you decide to postpone or drop out of the course. Your partner, your family, and sometimes your relationship with your employer, are not worth sacrificing for the sake of a qualification. You can take a degree at any time, but may not be able to find another partner, family or job like the one you have already. Obvious? Not if you're heavily stressed. A lot of students lose sight of this option when the stress levels are high. Sometimes postponing or leaving the course is the right choice. Knowing that you have this option can be a very reassuring safety net, and can help you get through bad times that are only temporary. Having said that, there's a difference between making a clear, informed decision to suspend or leave a course which isn't right for you, and giving up impulsively just because you happen to be having a bad day. If you're going through difficult circumstances, universities can be surprisingly accommodating and supportive in terms of offering ways for you to continue your degree when the emergency is over, and it's usually wiser to take this route, since it keeps your options open. If you do think you want to take time out or to leave the course completely, then don't make any drastic decisions about it for a week. If you still think it's the right decision after that week, then talk to your tutor about it, and take things from there.

MATURE STUDENTS

Specific problems

Some of the problems mature students with children encounter are specific, easily identifiable ones, which you'll discover soon enough. Here are some of the classics:

- You have a 9.00 am lecture which clashes with the school run.
- You have a lecture at 3.00 pm or later which clashes with the school run.
- All the car park spaces are taken by 9.30 am and you can't get in before 9.45 am because of the school run.
- You have a lecture at any time between 9.00 am and 6.00 pm during school holidays (including half terms).
- One of the children or an elderly parent is ill.

- There is a problem with the roof or the boiler and you need to stay home for the builder/plumber/electrician.
- There's a major family event such as Christmas and you have an assignment due in the day after you return to university.
- The children want your attention when there's an assignment to be completed by the next day.

The simplest first step to dealing with these is to share ideas with other mature students who have been through the same problem. What solutions have they found to the obvious problems about finding the right balance between noticing the children and doing the course; or making arrangements for when one of the children is ill? The university might helpfully arrange a talk about this for you, which often takes the form of a patronising lecture about time management from someone younger than you, who doesn't have children, and who knows much less about time management and priority management than you do. Since individual circumstances can vary widely, we can't offer foolproof solutions to these problems. However, the strategies we touched on earlier in the section on support networks and time planning, are key here. If you are likely to face the kind of problems listed above, before you start your degree, make sure you have a good network of family, friends and neighbours who have agreed to help you out with childcare, walking the dog, or waiting in for plumbers. Secondly, make sure the university staff you'll be working with are well aware of your other commitments. If you think you will need an extension to a deadline for an assignment, ask about it as soon as you realise it may be an issue, and be prepared to provide doctor's notes, letters from employers and so on, as evidence that you have had a real emergency which has prevented you completing on time. Consider the possibility of taking a degree a module at a time, an option offered by, for example, the Open University.

In addition, you're likely to find that the younger undergraduates alternate between treating you as a primordial relic who remembers the Roaring Twenties and treating you as a source of wisdom and support when things go wrong in their lives or when someone needs to be student representative and complain about the lecturer that everybody hates. How to handle this depends on your personality. Some people enjoy hamming it up and playing the primordial relic; others simply ignore the age thing and get on with life; others again get a feeling of accomplishment from helping the younger students to blossom and grow.

Less well-defined problems

There are also problems affecting mature students which are more insidious because you have difficulty putting your finger on them. Some classics are:

- feeling that you just don't quite fit in somehow
- wondering if you're wasting your time
- feeling that you don't understand how the academic world works, or feeling stupid
- wondering if you'll manage to stick the course till the end.

There are a couple of common themes underlying most of the general and the hard-to-identify problems mature students face. One them is knowing the rules of the academic game, the other is self-doubt in various forms. Self-doubt usually arises either because you are in an unfamiliar situation, and don't know whether you are up to the task, or because you have been in a similar situation before, and didn't do very well. If you have previously failed exams, for example, you may experience a feeling of sick dread every time you enter a lecture theatre. Obviously, you need to replace the negative feelings with more positive ones. How do you do this? One way is to take a long, objective look at why you failed your exams, or didn't finish a previous degree course. Was it because you didn't understand the work, didn't manage your time effectively, or were there specific circumstances involved that are no longer relevant? Make sure you have addressed the problems this time round by using the strategies described in this book, or by discussing your concerns with your tutor. If you have addressed the problems, but still feel your stomach muscles knotting up every time you walk through the front door of the department, a simple strategy of positive reinforcement can help erase the negative feelings. Treat yourself to a cappuccino or download a track onto your iPod after every lecture, for example. (Hopefully, the feelings will soon disappear, or this strategy could get expensive!)

If you're worried about coping with the work, try reading through your lecture notes every evening, to make sure you understand them, and read up on, or talk over things you don't understand with other students or your tutor. If you don't get a good mark for your first piece of written work, make sure you find out why, and try to address any problem areas with the next assignment. Facing up to your weaker skills is not a sign of incompetence, but an opportunity to get better.

We've said a fair amount about the rules of the game throughout this book, but it's worth returning to the topic here since some aspects of it are more of an issue for mature students. More specifically, there are some questions about the rules of the game which mature students wonder about much more often than younger ones. For starters, there's the issue of why it's called a 'game' at all. That can make the whole process sound trivial and ultimately pointless. Games in the sense of sports in fact tend to be treated as something deadly serious by their players, and are often a major factor in players' decisions about life events and lifestyles, but that's a secondary issue. The key point about the game metaphor is that games have rules, and if you've ever tried playing a game where you don't know all the rules, you can end up in an embarrassing mess. Almost all games have a scoring system: some games have simple rules, whereas others have lots of complex rules; there are no prizes for guessing which of these categories the academic game falls into. It is also a game where the other players expect you to know the rules already or to pick them up as you go along. No one is likely to teach them to you. That's enough to make anyone feel stressed, so here are some of the questions and the corresponding unwritten rules that frequently crop up with mature students.

Why does this stuff have so little visible connection to the real world?

This is a particularly common question among students who have previously been in employment. There are several answers. The main one is that universities deal with knowledge about the deep underlying principles, so that you can work out for yourself from those principles solutions to apply to real world situations. Universities are pretty good at this on the whole. They're usually less good at explaining the intermediate steps you need to take to turn the principles into a practical solution – they'll probably assume that once you've grasped the concept, you'll be able to work out the implications for yourself.

Why do they waste their time on such weird things?

The work of academics often looks utterly unconnected with anything. Sometimes the reason is personal curiosity. More often, though, it's to do with the reasons that difficult problems are difficult. Academics get more prestige and research funding if they crack difficult problems than if they crack easy ones. With difficult problems, it's a pretty good bet that the actual solution isn't the obvious one (because if the obvious solution is the right one, then the problem won't remain unsolved for long). If you combine this with the point about underlying principles, the result is that the search for the answer can lead into some very unlikely places. It usually makes sense when the chain of reasoning is spelled out, but most academics have too heavy a workload to spend time explaining their research to students on taught courses.

Why don't they give us better training?

This question goes to the heart of a long-running polite division in academia. In brief, universities typically view their role as being primarily about education, and colleges' role as being primarily about training. What's the difference? In brief, training tells you what to do, whereas education tells you (a) a little about what you need to do, (b) a moderate amount about why you need to do it and (c) a lot about how to work out for yourself some better ways of doing it. So, for example, a university psychology course would typically cover the theory underpinning various forms of therapeutic technique, whereas a further education college might train students on its counselling course, to use a particular style of psychotherapy. Each type of course is fine and worthy, but serves different purposes. If you're doing a university degree, then that means that you've signed up for education rather than just training, so listen and learn, even if you decide afterwards that you don't love it.

Problems affecting mature students who have spent time in the working world

Many of the classic problems affecting mature students who have previously been working also apply to mature students in general, and so have been covered above. There are, however, some specific problems which we deal with in this section. A classic difficulty is that you've changed from a senior member of staff in your previous organisation into a first year undergraduate, which is about as low as it gets on the academic status ladder. This can be seriously unsettling. It's not so bad if the lecturing staff show signs of recognising your situation, but if they don't, the transition can be stressful. A related problem is that you might find marked differences in values between academia and your previous role. The commonest manifestation of this is in writing style, which was covered in Chapter 4 on assessment. You're used to writing clear, concise text that goes to the heart of the matter; they expect you to write something that unpicks obscure details. You're used to finding quick practical solutions that work; they're used to tackling the deep underlying principles, on a timescale of years or even decades. You're used to slick PowerPoint presentations; you find yourself listening to a lecture from someone in shirtsleeves sitting on a desk who occasionally scribbles something on a whiteboard.

So what do you do about it? The things to remember are that you chose to do the degree, and that the degree is about learning new things. Academia usually has reasons for doing things the way it does. If you don't know why, then it's a good idea to find out by asking an approachable member of staff over an informal cup of coffee, and making an effort to understand what they're saying, rather than trying to persuade them that they're wrong. It may be a frustrating experience initially, because you're starting from very different places, but if you can learn both viewpoints, then it puts you in a very powerful position. Industry and commerce are usually very good at the things that they do routinely; academia is usually very good at the things that industry and commerce find difficult. If you can perform effectively in both academia and the world of work, this is a significant and very useful ability.

PART-TIME STUDENTS

Conflicting practical demands

One obvious problem that affects most part-time students is the conflict between the practical demands of the day job and the studies. People tend to start off optimistic about being able to handle this, basing their judgements on carefully calculated timetables or on guesstimates of how much time everything will take. In practice, this usually works well until the first minor crisis, at which point everything falls apart in a messy heap. The underlying cause of this is lack of what is known as 'slack' or 'spare capacity.' It's like having your finances neatly organised so that you always have a little bit more income than expenditure; that's fine until you hit a big bit of unexpected expenditure. If you have enough money saved up, then you're all right; if you haven't, you suddenly acquire a significant debt, which is going to take a long time to clear. It's exactly the same with time. If your day job unexpectedly requires extra time, or if you're ill for a week, then suddenly you don't have any slack, your boss is hassling you, and you're behind in a couple of assignments simultaneously. There are various things you can do to reduce the risk of these problems, and to reduce their severity if they do occur. One is to make sure from the start that your boss and family are willing to be supportive during your degree; if they aren't, then you need to think seriously about whether to take on the degree. Efficient time-budgeting and priority management can help. We've described these skills earlier in this chapter and in Chapter 8.

Conflicting emotional demands

A related issue is the conflicting emotional demands of home and work. Your family will want you to be emotionally involved in their highs and lows; your boss will want you to be a good team player who is emotionally supportive in the ups and downs of organisational life; Christmas and summer holidays are likely to be a nightmare of conflicting loyalties. Again, time-budgeting and priority management can help; assertiveness can be particularly helpful for this problem (see Chapter 2). If it all gets too much, then it's worth stepping back and looking at the problem in perspective. If you leave your family, it's a major life event that's the topic of great literature like *Anna Karenina*; if you leave your job, you will have no income, and there's a number of books about being penniless and hungry; but if you drop out of a degree course, the world of literature will not give a damn. Blood comes first; if the tension between job, family and degree gets too much, then family is most important, followed by income.

STUDENTS FROM OVERSEAS

Before you start

If you're a student from abroad, you'll have many interesting experiences with stress before you even reach the university. You'll need to complete the admissions forms, which are often difficult to understand even if English is your first language. You'll probably need to have your certificates validated, and maybe translated as well. It's a good idea to get help from people who already know the British university system and who know how to complete the forms. After this, there will also be the emotional times of preparing for the journey, and of saying goodbye to friends and family, followed by the exhaustion of the journey itself. If you're feeling stressed by all of this, rest assured you are not unique; it's a feeling that everybody in your position goes through. The exercises in the second chapter of this book and in the appendices should help; also, you may find the chapter for new students useful.

During the journey to the UK, you'll probably focus just on getting to your destination. You might remember the welcoming photos of the campus on the university's website, with images of smiling students in bright sunshine against a background of beautiful gardens. What you might forget is that those photos are usually taken in summer, and you'll probably be arriving in autumn. You'll also quite probably be arriving late because of delays on your journey. The result is that many overseas students arrive at their university late at night, in the dark, in the rain and the cold, when everywhere appears to be closed. It's not a pleasant experience. So, what can you do about it? The simplest solution is to find out what you should do when you get here *before* you begin your journey. You can ask the university administrators what to do if this happens to you. They should then tell you where the 24-hour reception is, where you will at least meet a human being who will welcome you. It's also wise to ask the administrators about where you could stay if you arrive at your destination very late – they should be able to tell you about nearby hotels where you can stay overnight, so that you can get a good night's sleep, and then arrive at the university the next morning, when offices are open and the world is a more pleasant place. It's a wise idea to make sure you have enough cash in Sterling with you to cover expenses of this sort – it will reduce the potential stress considerably. We realise that this advice possibly comes too late for many readers of this book, who will buy it after they've already arrived here, but if one of your friends is thinking of coming to a British university, it's something you might want to tell them about.

Arrival

Once you have arrived, you will need to get yourself registered at the university. British bureaucracy is fairly simple compared with bureaucracy in some other places, so it shouldn't stress you too much. The university system is used to dealing with overseas students, and is usually friendly and supportive. You'll also need to find your accommodation. Most universities offer places in university halls of residence to overseas students and to first year students. There are many advantages in this, and we've assumed that you'll be staying in a hall for at least your first year. If you aren't, you might find useful the section on accommodation in Chapter 5. The first week or two will probably be eventful, including good things as well as bad things. After that, you'll be reasonably familiar with the university system, and will probably have a routine for your weekdays. That's the point at which problems can begin. For the first two weeks many students are too busy to think much about their friends and family at home, or to feel lonely. Once there is some free time, and you are used to Britain, then you start to miss things from home, and to feel like a stranger in a strange land. You'll miss family and friends; you'll miss familiar food and familiar smells and sights; you'll miss little things that sound silly when you tell people about them, like a familiar bell that you used to hear every morning on the way to work. It's perfectly normal to feel this way – almost everyone feels like this in a new country. It can hurt a lot, but for most people it gets better after the first few weeks.

Cultural issues

There are other problems which arise occasionally, such as when you're away from home and missing a festival or a family event, like a birthday, that usually brings the family together. There will be little things that suddenly remind you of home, just when you think you're used to being in Britain. There will be things that happen here which suddenly remind you of how much difference there can be between cultures – for instance, an item in the local news, or an event at the university, which shocks you but which is treated as perfectly normal by the people around you.

Some overseas students react by finding other students from their home country and spending as much time as possible with them. This is understandable, but it isn't a good idea. It means that you won't be making good use of being in the UK at a British university. You might as well have studied at a university back home. It can also cause problems if your English isn't very good. Your exams will be in English, so you need to practise it as much as possible and speak it as well as possible. A better strategy is to have a mixture of friends. For example, you might have one evening a week when you socialise with students from your homeland, and another evening when you socialise with students from the UK. It's a good idea to find the university support services for overseas students, and to ask them what facilities are available to help you. There are usually societies for students from the same country, or from the same religion, and these will be able to give you friendship, advice and support. This is particularly useful for learning about differences in culture between your country and the UK, so that you don't accidentally cause offence or get into trouble.

Being an overseas student can be particularly difficult if you're a mature student with a partner and children and a senior post back home, but find yourself living in a hall of residence surrounded by noisy teenagers. Universities are often understanding about this situation. Some have special accommodation for mature students in a quiet area, so if this applies to you, then it's a good idea to ask the university whether they can offer accommodation somewhere more suited to your needs.

A frequent problem if you are a student from overseas is that you can't be familiar with all the social conventions in your new home, so you may worry about unintentionally sending out the wrong social signals to other people. A useful strategy is to make friends with at least one sensible, friendly British student of the same sex as yourself, and to ask them for advice when you're not sure about something.

There's one last problem which often affects overseas students just when they think that the stress is over. When you return home after a course at a British university, you'll probably have changed without realising it. You may have adopted some forms of British culture, and have got used to some British conventions. You'll also have experienced things that people in your home community haven't experienced. The result is that you may at times feel like a stranger in your own land. Again, this is perfectly normal, given what has happened to you, but it's a strange feeling. You may find it useful to find other ex-students who have been through the same experience, so that you can talk about it with someone who understands how you feel.

OTHER STUDENTS: TEMPORARY ABSENCES

There are various other types of student who are likely to face problems sooner or later because they don't fit neatly into The System. The issue might be an academic one, such as students doing a year abroad or a sandwich year. Or you may have had time out of your course due to illness or through switching courses in mid-stream. At a practical level, this can lead to being 'out of sync' with the regulations, if the university has changed some of its rules while you were away and has forgotten to allow for students who have been temporarily out of the system. There are similar issues if you've done a course or module that doesn't map neatly onto The System, such as modules you did on your year abroad which don't have an exact equivalent at home. At an emotional level, returning after time away can feel very odd. The places will look comfortingly familiar, but there will be a weird absence which is difficult to pin down at first. It's the absence of 'familiar strangers' – people that you see every day, although you may never have spoken to them. Many of them will have graduated and left during your year away. The result is that you can feel like a ghost, passing unnoticed through crowded places.

You can also feel like an outsider for non-academic reasons, such as being a member of a minority group, whether it's sexual, ethnic, religious or political. Ironically, a university is one of the best places to be in terms of social support if you're in a minority – you'll probably find it easier to meet others like you at university than anywhere else, and you're much more likely to be accepted in a university than in most other places. If this is the case for you, then you should find out about the university's support systems, clubs, and so on: you might be pleasantly surprised.

SUMMARY

If you're a mature student, an overseas student, a part-time student or are otherwise different from the standard-issue full-time home-grown undergraduate aged between 18 and 22, then you're likely to feel marginalised at university. If you have a family or a job, then you'll experience stresses from conflicting demands for your time and attention. You may also experience stress from starting again at the bottom of the status ladder as a new student. You'll also probably encounter culture clash between the academic world and your usual world. If you go through these feelings, that's normal, and we describe some ways of handling them; it's worth persevering, because the students reading this chapter are likely both to get the most out of a degree and also to give back most to the academic world. They're also likely to be the students most valued by the academic staff, even if the academics don't always show it until graduation day.

BIBLIOGRAPHY AND SUGGESTED FURTHER RESOURCES

The Open University has a lot of experience of mature students and part-time students; if you belong to one or both of those categories, it's well worth looking at their support material, and investigating their website.

Linda Pritchard and Leila Roberts's *The Mature Student's Guide to Higher Education* (Open University Press/McGraw-Hill Education, 2006) is what its title says. It works through the process of undertaking higher education, including career options at the end of your course.

If you are an overseas student, then you will probably find your university's student support material to be more useful than general books about studying in the UK. Most universities have online material which answers specific frequently asked questions such as 'How can I get from the airport to the university?' If your university doesn't answer a more general question, such as 'How do I apply for a student visa?' then another university's website might.

APPENDIX 1   Emergencies

Are you having a panic attack – feeling terrified, faint, with shallow breathing and clammy skin? If so:

- Sit down – if there's no chair, sit on the floor.
- Breathe in slowly, counting slowly to four.
- Hold your breath, counting slowly to four.
- Breathe out slowly, counting slowly to four.
- Hold your breath, counting slowly to four.
- Repeat.

Is there blood involved?

If either you or someone else has been injured, raped, or otherwise traumatised, then:

- Stabilise the immediate situation (get yourself or the person involved into a safe place and stop any serious bleeding).
- If you're starting to panic, breathe slowly and deeply, counting slowly to four on each breath, and pausing for a few seconds between breaths.
- Call for proper help – if in doubt, call 999 and explain the situation to the operator.
- If you are feeling physically shocked (cold, shaky, faint, dizzy or can't think clearly) keep yourself warm, eat or drink something sweet to raise your blood sugar levels, and find someone to be with you.

APPENDIX 2 Resources

Useful phone numbers. Make a list like this and put in an easy-to-find place (such as a personal organiser, on your mobile and/or stuck on the wall by the phone)

24 hour counselling	
Doctor	
Rape Crisis Centre	
Chemists	
Local police station	
Hospital	
NHS direct (medical advice)	
Dentist	
Emergency dentist	
Landlord	
Electricity emergency	
Gas emergency	
Plumber	
Electrician	
Gas fitter	
Locksmith	
Glazier	
Student support	
Student union	
Finance office	
Admissions office	
College/University	

APPENDIX 3 Immediate relaxation exercises

This appendix contains more relaxation exercises, following on from those in Chapter 2.

Immediate relaxation: Relaxation in a crisis

When you're in a situation that is stressing you out, this exercise will give you some immediate relief:

- Take a deep breath in and hold it for as long as it takes to say 'hold it' four times.

- Then, while you breathe out slowly:

  drop your shoulders
  silently and slowly say 'CALM' to yourself.

- Take two normal, slow breaths.

- Repeat.

This exercise is most effective if you do it with your eyes closed, but will still work even if you are talking to someone, are in a meeting or driving. If you're in one of those situations, do the exercise with your *eyes open*.

If you find tension builds up during the day, repeat the exercise a few times every hour. If you get tense whilst driving or being driven, do it at every set of traffic lights or each traffic island. If you get stressed during meetings or talking on the phone, do it before you speak. Before an important meeting or a confrontation, go to the bathroom and repeat the exercise four times with your eyes closed. You won't have time to become deeply relaxed, but it could really help to reduce tension in moments of pressure.

Immediate relaxation: Square breathing

This will help you sleep or calm down in just a few minutes:

> - Breathe in, counting 1, 2.
> - Hold your breath and count 3, 4.
> - Breathe out counting 5, 6.
> - Hold on empty and count 7, 8.
> - Repeat.

This is relaxing partly because you do it to slow down and breathe deeply. It also makes you concentrate on the counting and acts as a thought-blocking tactic against intrusive thoughts, as it requires focus.

Immediate relaxation: Quick tension release

This exercise will help whenever you feel panicky, anxious or uptight:

> - Let your breath out. (Don't breathe in first.)
> - Take in a slow, gentle breath; hold it for a second.
> - Let it go, with a leisurely sigh of relief.
> - Drop your shoulders and relax your hands.
> - If your jaw is tense, unclench your teeth.
> - If you have to speak, speak more slowly and in a lower tone of voice.

Immediate relaxation: Anchoring

This is a technique we've borrowed from Neuro-Linguistic Programming (NLP). There's debate about the validity of NLP as a whole, but it contains some exercises which many people find very effective. The exercise of Anchoring gives you rapid access to a state of calmness.

First, relax deeply (see Appendix 5). Then, when you are deeply relaxed, touch your thumb and middle finger together and squeeze slightly. If you repeatedly combine this simple action with the feeling of being deeply relaxed, you will learn to associate the state of relaxation with the action of touching thumb and middle finger together. For quick relaxation, just repeat the squeezing action and you will relax significantly, without anyone ever knowing you were getting tense.

APPENDIX 4   Exercises to help you sleep

Stress is often accompanied by insomnia and poor quality sleep. The following exercises help sleep, and improve quality of sleep.

Exercise: Breathing to help sleep

- Lie in the position in which you want to sleep.
- Focus on your breathing.
- Whilst breathing out, focus on relaxation.
- For the first three exhalations, focus on the feeling of your body against the bed.
- Continue to breathe, while focusing on relaxation, letting all your muscles go limp, noting the sinking and slowing down sensations.
- Once totally relaxed, visualise your breath as coloured vapour and see the air flowing into and out of your body.
- Continue to focus on your breathing and the relaxed feeling.

This exercise should result in you falling gently asleep.

Exercise: Imagery to help sleep

Visualise a black, velvety board. See your finger writing your full name, very slowly and neatly in white across the board. Every time you make a mistake, start again.

APPENDIX 5   Deep relaxation techniques

The previous appendices contain techniques that are useful for fixing immediate problems with feeling stressed. This appendix contains techniques for deep relaxation, which many people find useful as part of their regular routine.

Deep relaxation: Autogenic relaxation

Autogenic relaxation helps balance those of the body's self-regulating systems which form part of the fight-or-flight response. They are triggered when you are stressed. Blood pressure, heart rate and breathing rate increase as you react to stress. Autogenic relaxation helps you to control stress by training the autonomic nervous system to be more relaxed when you are not faced with a genuine need to run or fight. It is a way of training the subconscious mind to create a state of inner calm. Autogenic training emphasises smooth rhythmic breathing, regular calm heartbeat and pleasant warmth with relaxing heaviness throughout the body.

By matching an image of a regular, repetitive movement with your breathing and slowing down the pace of the movement and your breathing, the other parts of the autogenic system follow that pace. We have used the image of ocean waves here, but you could imagine yourself sitting on a swing, snorkelling in warm water, or kneading bread dough. Any form of regular, repetitive movement will do. Allow at least ten minutes to become deeply relaxed.

---

1   DEEP BREATHING

- Imagine ocean waves rolling in . . . and out. Match your breathing to the rhythm.
- Silently say: 'My breathing is smooth and rhythmic.'

2   HEARTBEAT REGULATION EXERCISES

- Imagine slow ocean waves.
- Silently say: 'My heartbeat is calm and regular.'

3   BLOOD FLOW
   (A) Right hand and arm

- Silently say: 'My right arm and hand are heavy and warm.'
- Imagine the warm sun shining down on you.

   (B) Left hand and arm

- Silently say, 'My left hand and arm are heavy and warm.'
- Imagine the sunshine warming your arm.

   (C) Legs and feet

- Silently say: 'My legs and feet are heavy and warm.'
- Imagine the warmth flowing down from your arms and hands and gently flowing into your legs and feet.

4   WHEN YOU FEEL RELAXED
Say to yourself: 'I am calm' and gently squeeze your middle finger and thumb together to anchor the state of relaxation.

5   WHEN YOU ARE READY
Count forward from one to three slowly, and gently open your eyes. The world will seem calmer and slowed down.

Deep relaxation. Breathing exercise

- Sit quietly in a comfortable position.
- Close your eyes.
- Deeply relax all your muscles, beginning at your feet and progressing up to your face.
- Breathe through your nose. Think about your breathing. As you breathe out say the word 'ONE' silently to yourself. For example, breathe IN … OUT, 'ONE', IN … OUT, 'ONE' and so on. Breathe easily and naturally.
- Continue for about ten minutes. When you finish, sit quietly for a few minutes, at first with your eyes closed, then with your eyes open. Do not stand up quickly or you may feel dizzy.
- Let relaxation happen at its own pace. If distracting thoughts come into your mind push them gently away and say 'ONE.'

Practising this for a few minutes once or twice a day will result in your feeling increasingly calm.

Calm, aware relaxation exercise

Appendix 1 contains exercises for immediate relaxation when stressed; Appendix 3 contains exercises for deeper relaxation, which can be used as part of a regular routine for maintaining a more balanced life. Both of these involve inward focusing. The techniques here offer ways of relaxing while being aware of the surrounding world.

Listen to music from the Baroque period or other calm, rhythmic music

Baroque music was written in the first half of the eighteenth century by composers such as Corelli, Telemann, Bach, Haydn, Albinoni and Vivaldi; many people find that listening to it produces calm and relaxation. The Baroque composers attempted to create an ideal mathematical form and harmony in their music. They produced music with a rhythm and structure which tends to promote a state of calm, relaxed awareness. Baroque music tends to use a consistent musical theme, and it explores symmetry and pattern. The object of the exercise was to produce a unifying mood and liberate the mind from earthly concerns. (The rhythm is very precise; many stress counsellors use pieces with 60 beats per minute to produce an increase in calming theta and alpha waves in the brain.)

Thought-watching

This technique is what it sounds like; you observe your own thoughts, including daydreams and worrying about problems. The action of observing requires deliberate thought about something other than the daydreams and worries, and the deliberate thought will help you break out of the negative emotions.

Index